Becoming a
CASEWORKER

Cassandra L. Bransford, PhD

LEARNINGEXPRESS®

NEW YORK

Library of Congress Cataloging-in-Publication Data
    Bransford, Cassandra L.
    Becoming a caseworker / Cassandra L. Bransford.—1st ed.
        p. cm.
    Includes bibliographical references.
    ISBN: 978-1-57685-614-7 (pbk. : alk. paper)
    1. Social work education—United States—Problems, exercises, etc.
    2. Social service—United States—Problems, exercises, etc.   3. Social workers—
    training of—United States.   4. Social case work—United States.   I. Title.
    HV11.5.B73   2008
    361.3—dc22

                                                            2008000054

Printed in the United States of America

9 8 7 6 5 4 3 2 1

First Edition

ISBN: 978-1-57685-614-7

For more information or to place an order, contact LearningExpress at:
    55 Broadway
    8th Floor
    New York, NY 10006

Or visit us at:
    www.learnatest.com

Contents

Contents

Acknowledgments and Dedication

I'D LIKE to thank all of the caseworkers, social workers, and students who contributed to the creation of this book. A special thanks to Gwen Chaffin, Sally Ryan, Christy Bianconi, Brian Flynn, Barb Barry, and Ann Dolan for sharing their personal stories of what it means to be a caseworker.

This book is dedicated to the recipients of casework services, who, through their struggles, courage, and perseverance, provide continuing inspiration and hope to us all.

Introduction to Casework

SO, YOU'RE thinking about becoming a caseworker? Casework is a career unlike any other. It is a career where you work to help others achieve a better, more satisfying life.

As a caseworker, you might help a child overcome feelings of low self-esteem or perform better academically in school. You might assist an immigrant family in adjusting to life in a new country, or provide support to a homebound elder. You might help a single mother find adequate housing for herself and her children, or assist a young adult in transitioning from foster care to living independently. There are many opportunities for those who choose to pursue the very challenging and rewarding career path of casework. In fact, this field is expected to grow significantly over the next decade and beyond.

This book is an introduction to casework and its role in the field of human services. It is written for those who may be interested in pursuing casework as a professional career. In addition to identifying just who caseworkers are and what they do, this book will also serve as a how-to resource for those who may choose to begin the rewarding journey of becoming a caseworker.

Within the social or human services occupations, many different titles are used to describe the roles that workers have to help others. These titles evolved over time and include, among others, friendly visitor, case-worker, social worker, and case manager. By acquainting you with the meaning behind these titles, the educational and certification requirements necessary to fulfill specific occupations, and the roles these titles have across a wide range of agency-based practice, this book will help you to better decide on a direction for your career in social or human services.

If you are interested in making a difference in the world, and are looking for a gratifying career where you can help others, as well as grow personally and professionally, then casework may be just the right career for you.

THE MANY ROLES OF CASEWORKERS

Caseworkers see individuals who face life-threatening diseases, mental health issues, inadequate housing, poverty, unemployment, serious illness or disability, substance abuse, and, increasingly, natural and man-made disasters. Caseworkers also assist families that have serious domestic conflicts, sometimes involving physical abuse of children or spouses, or that are undergoing the strain of divorce or caring for elderly parents or grandparents with Alzheimer's disease.

Caseworkers may also counsel and aid individuals and families who require social service assistance, such as food stamps, Medicaid, and government-supported housing. They may assess whether families are eligible for entitlement programs. They may investigate cases of alleged child abuse or neglect, or conduct home studies to determine suitability for foster home placement or adoption. In sum, caseworkers provide services to a variety of individuals and families from diverse backgrounds in a myriad of settings.

Additionally, caseworkers work across a range of fields of practice. For example, caseworkers may be employed in the areas of child welfare, criminal justice, developmental disabilities, gerontology, domestic violence, health care, and mental health and substance abuse.

Academic programs that prepare individuals to become caseworkers are available at all educational levels, from associate's degrees to master's of social work (MSW) degrees. A minimum of an associate's degree in human services is usually required for obtaining a position as a social services assistant or beginning caseworker. Often, caseworkers are required to have a bachelor's degree in social work (BSW) or a related field, although localities and the social and human service organizations located within them vary considerably in terms of the credentials required for becoming a caseworker.

A master's degree in social work can provide opportunities for advancement into specialized positions in both private and government agency-based practice. Currently, many state boards of social work are lobbying for title protection, which seeks to restrict the designation of the title of "social worker" only to those individuals who have achieved a BSW or MSW social work degree from an institution accredited by the Council of Social Work Education.

Depending upon where you live, the degrees and certifications necessary to become a caseworker will vary. For example, the New York State Service Examination in Casework for Oneida County (see Appendix C) requires that individuals have either a combination of a bachelor's degree with 12 credit hours of coursework in social work, sociology, psychology, or childhood development or a bachelor's degree and one year of experience in social casework in order to take the caseworker examination.

Some states require that in addition to a varied combination of academic degree and level of experience, individuals wishing to become caseworkers must also pass a civil service examination to obtain publicly funded casework positions. Other states require that prospective caseworkers must pass first pass licensing or certification requirements. Indeed, a push for all states to adopt licensing requirements is currently underway within the profession of social work.

OVERVIEW OF BOOK

In order to assist you in learning more about casework and the many areas of specialization available to those who choose to pursue a career in this very challenging and rewarding field, this book is divided into the following chapters:

Chapter One provides an introduction to the field of casework. It explains why you might want to choose to become a caseworker, and discusses such important topics as job satisfaction, growth potential, salary, and benefits. Chapter One also describes the general skills required to become a caseworker, the types of positions available within casework, and the diversity of settings in which caseworkers may be employed.

Chapter Two reviews in expanded detail the specific skills that caseworkers use across settings and in their respective social work roles, including, for example, establishing and maintaining effective helping relationships, procedures for conducting an initial interview, techniques for establishing rapport, cultural competence in working with a diverse clientele, ethical principles and decision-making processes, confidentiality issues, duty to inform, current HIPAA regulations, and record-keeping procedures.

Chapter Three introduces you to specific areas of caseworker knowledge, including public health casework, casework with children, and housing and welfare assistance eligibility casework.

In **Chapter Four**, you will learn all about casework/social work education programs, and how to choose an educational program and an institution that is right for you. Information is provided about the different degrees and concentrations that are available, what kinds of courses you might expect to take, how to increase your chances of getting admitted into particular programs, and employment opportunities following graduation. For example, you will learn about varying licensing and certification requirements across the country. The kinds of questions that are generally asked on civil service examinations are also discussed and reviewed.

Appendix A provides a list and description of the most important and relevant professional organizations in the area of casework that are available for membership and the benefits of joining particular organizations. **Appendix B** provides you with a directory of online and print resources that may be useful to caseworkers. **Appendix C** includes sample announcements for examinations in casework, as well as sample descriptions of open positions. **Appendix D** provides examples of academic curricula for programs in human services and social work.

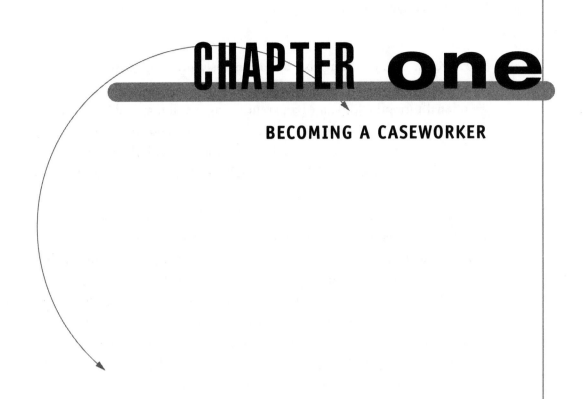

CHAPTER one

BECOMING A CASEWORKER

ARE YOU the kind of person who enjoys helping others? Are you a good listener? Do you like working with people? Are you detail-oriented and able to multitask? Do you like a challenge? Are you interested in learning about people from different backgrounds and cultures? Would you like to help improve the lives of individuals and families?

If so, then you might consider becoming a caseworker. Casework can be a tremendously rewarding and gratifying career. As you assist people in improving the quality of their lives, support clients in obtaining the necessary resources to take better care of themselves and their families, work toward overcoming disparities in healthcare and educational opportunities, and strive for a more equitable and socially just world, you will likely feel a great sense of pride and accomplishment.

However, casework can also be enormously draining. Listening to the stories of people suffering from domestic violence, bearing witness to the emotional turmoil and pain of a parent losing a child, attending to the intense needs of the ill or infirm, or dealing with individuals who are going through any number of unexpected crises, disasters, and life transitions can be difficult, and, at times, overwhelming. The caseloads can be high, and a great deal of paperwork is required.

Historically, many casework jobs have been public sector jobs. Caseworkers are often hired by county departments of social services to provide assistance to clients in need of public assistance, housing, jobs, or other public services. County jobs generally offer good salaries and benefit packages.

Some individuals who have no compelling desire to work with poor or potentially needy clients may take jobs as caseworkers simply in order to obtain job security and good benefit packages. For those individuals who are not truly committed to helping others, the potential for burnout can be high. The work can be frustrating and, at times, unsafe.

Individuals seeking casework services are often angry, and with good reason. They may be hungry and cold. They may need food or clothing for themselves and their children. They may be facing eviction, or already be homeless. They may have no heat or electricity, or be dealing with unscrupulous landlords who do not properly maintain properties. They may be living with abusive and violent spouses or partners, and may have no support systems. Many clients feel a sense of hopelessness and fear about their futures, for both themselves and their families.

Moreover, clients may have had unsatisfactory experiences with caseworkers in the past, and consequently, they assume that you will be no different. Indeed, there are times when you cannot provide the help you may wish to provide or that a client may need. Many bureaucratic rules must be followed, and, if caseworkers are not careful, they can end up as alienated bureaucrats—emotionally distant and simply going through the motions of their jobs without any real concern for the individuals and families they are serving.

On the other hand, there can be no greater feeling of satisfaction or reward than helping a displaced mother and her young children find housing, or helping a young man with few job prospects enter a job training program and finally secure a decent job with living wages so that he may support his family, or making sure food and healthcare are provided to a homebound elder.

Gwen Chaffin, a 59-year-old former caseworker returning to school to earn a master's in social work at Binghamton University, describes her experience working as an Income Maintenance Worker in both Prince George's County in Maryland and Onondaga County in upstate New York:

> *"When you work at the Department of Social Services (DSS), you have to be caring, concerned, and respectful. The reason for that is because when people come in, they are dealing with what they consider to be an emergency. Our job is to help them through the problem."*

Gwen further remembers a time when a man specifically asked for her to help him with his case:

> *"I remember a man came in and he said, 'I want to see you. So and so said that you were fair. You might not be able to help me out, but you were fair.'"*

Gwen spoke about the rewards of being a caseworker:

> *"It feels good to help people. But you need to go in with an open mind. It's a hard job. You are going to do the best you can. . . . Sometimes clients get mad, frustrated, and upset. You may want to help them then, but the waiting period for services is 45 days. It's hard if you have children, no place to live. You must go in with compassion. There was a lady who came in. She had three children. She was running away from her boyfriend. He was beating on her. She didn't have a place to stay. I was able to find her a bed in a hotel for a few days, and then a place at the Salvation Army. I was able to expedite things. It was good for me . . . a great experience."*

Gwen also spoke about the frustrations of being a caseworker:

> *"I had a client call me. I was helping him find housing. He called me about 10 minutes before he was to be picked up by his parole officer. He*

had missed curfew, and had no place to put his furniture. Because of the time constraints, I wasn't able to assist him. He said, 'They're going to take me to jail. What am I going to do?' I couldn't help him. I said, 'There must be someone else you can call.' He didn't have anyone else to call. As a DSS worker, your hands are tied. There are rule books. You have your rules, in terms of how you work. New York State has regulations."

She summed up her thoughts about casework, as follows:

"You can't take a job like this and be judgmental. You never know when it could happen to you. You can't do the job if you don't have compassion. Some people take the job because they like the benefits. Burnout is high. The work can be frustrating. There are so many rules and regulations. Someone comes in needing assistance and you may have to tell them they're not eligible anymore. Some people come in and they're automatically told 'no.'"

THE HISTORICAL ROOTS OF CASEWORK

Casework, the oldest and most clearly elaborated field of social work practice, has its earliest roots in the humanitarian and charitable work of the late nineteenth century. At that time, private charity volunteers, many of them women, sought to provide support and assistance to families who were impoverished and suffering from a variety of ailments and misfortunes. In its earliest inception, social work sought to work with individuals and families to remedy their moral deficiencies, which were thought to be the cause of their misfortunes. However, as a consequence of the progressive movement in America between 1890 and 1913, and the proliferation of scientific methods as a preferred way of finding cures for medical ailments, social work began to look for systematic ways of providing help to the needy. Thus, casework was born.

In 1917, Mary Richmond, an early pioneer in the field of social work, wrote the first textbook on casework, *Social Diagnosis*. Within this book, she sought to apply a systematic and scientifically-based set of procedures and methods for providing help to those who were shut out of the mainstream, increasingly due to processes of industrialization. These individuals and families included the poor, the elderly, people with disabilities, immigrants, the mentally ill, widows, orphans, and other vulnerable people. The publication of *Social Diagnosis* marked the beginning of the transformation of charity workers into professional caseworkers.

Casework may be defined by its embrace of "a body of knowledge derived from the foundation sciences and from empirical experience; a scientific method or particular approach to phenomena; and a set of scientific attitudes including the open-mindedness and objectivity which reflect the spirit of scientific inquiry" (Germain 1970, 7). Casework thus sought to bring together a scientific approach with the pursuit of humanitarian social values in its quest to widen opportunities and support the well-being and functioning of individuals and families.

WHAT IS SOCIAL WORK?

Social work is a profession for those with a strong desire to help improve people's lives and also to improve the world that people live in, based upon the mission and values set forth in the National Association of Social Workers (NASW) code of ethics. On its website, the NASW, the official social work membership group, defines social work practice as consisting of:

> The professional application of social work values, principles, and techniques to one or more of the following ends: helping people obtain tangible services; counseling and psychotherapy with individuals, families, and groups; helping communities or groups provide or improve social and health services; and participating in legislative processes. The practice of social work requires knowledge of human development and behavior; of social and economic, and cultural institutions; and of the interaction of all these factors (NASW n.d., paragraph 1).

NASW has further defined the mission of social work as follows:

> The primary mission of the social work profession is to enhance human well-being and help meet the basic human needs of all people, with particular attention to the needs and empowerment of people who are vulnerable, oppressed, and living in poverty. A historic and defining feature of social work is the profession's focus on individual well-being in a social context and the well-being of society. Fundamental to social work is attention to the environmental forces that create, contribute to, and address problems in living (NASW 1999, paragraph 1).

Although some social workers may choose to work primarily on policy development or conducting research, those who provide direct service to individuals and families in agency-based or other organizational settings are called caseworkers. Caseworkers help individuals and families learn how to cope better with environmental problems, manage life transitions, deal with crises, provide clients with community and state resources, resolve interpersonal communication difficulties, and solve personal and family problems. Depending upon your level of education and training, and the type of position and setting that you are seeking, the job stresses may be greater or lesser.

For example, caseworkers hired as social and human service assistants, who have generally completed an associate's degree, typically receive lower pay and fewer opportunities for advancement than caseworkers who have pursued higher levels of education. They may also have higher caseloads and less organizational support or supervision. For those who choose to pursue bachelor's level or master's education, the compensation will be considerably better and the opportunities for advancement will increase significantly.

OUTLOOK AND EARNINGS FOR CASEWORKERS

Information in this section was obtained from the U.S. Department of Labor, Bureau of Labor Statistics. Retrieved September 28, 2007, from http://stats .bls.gov/oco/ocos059.htm and http://stats.bls.gov/oco/ocos060.htm.

Job Outlook for Caseworkers Employed as Social and Human Service Assistants

According to the U.S. Department of Labor, job opportunities for social and human service assistants are projected to grow much faster than the average for all occupations, ranking this field among the most rapidly growing. Although competition for jobs in urban areas will be greater than in rural areas, current funding trends in rural mental health and aging suggest that more opportunities will be available in rural areas, as well. Faced with rapid growth in the demand for social and human services, many employers increasingly rely on social and human service assistants to deliver services to clients.

Opportunities are expected to be strongest in private social service agencies, which provide services such as adult day care, meal delivery, and transportation programs. Employment in private agencies will grow as state and local governments continue to contract out services to the private sector in an effort to cut costs.

Demand for social services with aging adults will increase, as baby boomers (born between 1946 and 1964) enter into old age and will likely need these services, especially with the projected increased life expectancy. Additionally, more social and human service assistants will be needed to provide services to youth and adolescents, the homeless, the mentally disabled and developmentally challenged, and substance abusers. Some private agencies have been employing more social and human service assistants in place of social workers, who are generally more educated and, thus, more highly paid.

Social and human service workers will also be needed for job training programs. As social welfare policies shift the focus from benefit-based programs to work-based initiatives, demand will increase for people who can teach job skills to the people who are new to, or returning to, the workforce.

Residential care establishments will also be faced with increased pressures to respond to the needs of mentally and physically disabled persons. Since the mid-1970s, many of these patients live within residential care communities because they have been deinstitutionalized and lack the knowledge or the ability to care for themselves. Also, more community-based and supportive independent-living programs are expected to be established to house and provide assistance to the homeless, the mentally and physically disabled, and those who are returning to community life after incarceration. Moreover, the rise in veterans returning from military service will continue to provide job opportunities in the fields of mental health and vocational training. As the current trends in criminal justice are diverting substance abusers from jails and prisons to treatment programs, the employment of social and human service assistants in substance abuse treatment programs will also grow.

The number of jobs for social and human service assistants in local governments will grow, but not as fast as employment for social and human service assistants in other industries. Employment in the public sector may fluctuate with the level of funding provided by state and local governments.

Earnings of Social and Human Service Assistants

As of May 2006, social and human service assistants, who typically hold an associate's or bachelor's degree in human services or social work, earned a median annual salary of $25,580. The middle 50% earned between $20,350 and $32,440. The top 10% earned more than $40,780, while the lowest 10% earned less than $16,180.

Median annual earnings in the industries employing the largest numbers of social and human service assistants in May 2006 were:

State government	$30,510
Local government	29,810
Individual and family services	24,490
Vocational rehabilitation services	22,530
Residential mental retardation, mental health, and substance abuse facilities	22,380

Job Outlook for Social Workers Employed as Caseworkers

Employment of social workers is expected to increase faster than average (average is 9–17%) for all occupations through 2016. The rapidly growing elderly population and the aging baby boom generation will create greater demand for health and social services, resulting in particularly rapid job growth among gerontology social workers. Many job openings will also stem from the need to replace social workers who leave the occupation.

Competition for social worker jobs is expected to be highest in cities, where demand for services often is higher and training programs for social workers are prevalent. However, opportunities should also be good in rural areas, where it is often difficult to attract and retain qualified staff. By specialty, job prospects may be best for those social workers with a background in child welfare, gerontology, or substance abuse treatment.

As hospitals continue to limit the length of patient stays, the demand for social workers in hospitals will grow more slowly than in other areas. Because hospitals are releasing patients earlier than in the past, social worker employment in home healthcare services is growing. However, the expanding senior population is an even larger factor. Employment opportunities for social workers with backgrounds in gerontology should be good in the growing numbers of assisted-living and senior-living communities. The expanding senior population will also spur demand for social workers in nursing homes, long-term care facilities, and hospices.

Strong demand is expected for substance abuse social workers over the 2006–2016 projection periods. Substance abusers are increasingly being placed into treatment programs instead of being sentenced to prison. Because of the increasing numbers of individuals sentenced to prison or probation who are substance abusers, correctional systems are increasingly requiring substance abuse treatment as a condition added to their sentencing or probation. As this trend grows, demand will increase for treatment programs and social workers to assist abusers on the road to recovery.

Employment of social workers in private social service agencies will also increase. However, agencies increasingly will restructure services and hire lower paid social and human service assistants instead of social workers. Employment in state and local government agencies may grow somewhat in response to increasing needs for public welfare, family services, and child protection services; however, many of these services will be contracted out to private agencies, which compete with other private agencies on a time-limited, contractual time frame for funding, thus creating job instability for less educated workers. Employment levels in public and private social services agencies fluctuate, depending on need and government funding levels.

Employment of school social workers also is expected to grow as expanded efforts to respond to rising student enrollments and continued emphasis on integrating disabled children into the general school population lead to more jobs. There could be competition for school social work jobs in some areas because of the limited number of openings. The availability of federal, state, and local funding will be a major factor in determining the actual job growth in schools.

Opportunities for social workers in private practice will expand, but growth may be somewhat hindered by restrictions that managed care organizations put on mental health services. The growing popularity of employee assistance programs is expected to spur demand for private practitioners, some of whom provide social work services to corporations on a contractual basis. However, the popularity of employee assistance programs will fluctuate with the business cycle, because businesses are not likely to offer these services during recessions.

Earnings of Social Work Caseworkers

Median annual earnings of child, family, and school social workers were $37,480 in May 2006. The middle 50 percent earned between $29,590 and $49,060. The lowest 10 percent earned less than $24,480, and the top 10 percent earned more than $62,530. Median annual earnings in the industries employing the largest numbers of child, family, and school social workers in May 2006 were:

Elementary and secondary schools	$48,360
Local government	43,500
State government	39,000
Individual and family services	32,680
Other residential care facilities	32,590

Median annual earnings of medical and public health social workers were $43,040 in May 2006. The middle 50 percent earned between $34,110 and

$53,740. The lowest 10 percent earned less than $27,280, and the top 10 percent earned more than $64,070. Median annual earnings in the industries employing the largest numbers of medical and public health social workers in May 2006 were:

General medical and surgical hospitals	$48,420
Home healthcare services	44,470
Local government	41,590
Nursing care facilities	38,550
Individual and family services	35,510

Median annual earnings of mental health and substance abuse social workers were $35,410 in May 2006. The middle 50 percent earned between $27,940 and $45,720. The lowest 10 percent earned less than $22,490, and the top 10 percent earned more than $57,630. Median annual earnings in the industries employing the largest numbers of mental health and substance abuse social workers in May 2006 were:

Local government	$39,240
Psychiatric and substance abuse hospitals	39,550
Individual and family services	30,590
Residential mental retardation, mental health, and substance abuse facilities	34,290
Outpatient mental health and substance abuse facilities	34,920

Median annual earnings of social workers in all other areas were $43,580 in May 2006. The middle 50 percent earned between $32,530 and $56,420. The lowest 10 percent earned less than $25,540, and the top 10 percent earned more than $68,500. Median annual earnings in the industries employing the largest numbers of social workers in all other areas in May 2006 were:

Local government	$46,330
State government	45,070
Individual and family services	35,150

About one out of five social workers is a member of a union. Many belong to the unions associated with their places of employment.

Survey of Social Work Income by National Association of Social Workers[1]

According to a randomized survey conducted by the National Association of Social Workers (NASW 2003a), the median annual income of social workers was $44,400 in 2001. Full-time social workers employed in private, for-profit organizations received a median income of $56,700. Those social workers who were employed in nonprofit sectarian organizations, on the other hand, reported a median salary of $41,300. Among public employment opportunities, the federal government (including the military) is slightly more favorable than either state or local units of government.

Additionally, the survey found that social work salaries increased progressively as social workers become more experienced practitioners. For example, the survey found that the median salary for those with two to four years' experience was $35,600 in 2001. For social workers with 25 years experience or more, the median salary rose to $60,000.

WHAT CASEWORKERS DO AND WHERE THEY DO IT

Caseworkers provide direct services to individuals and families in a variety of settings and work with many types of people. They work in hospitals, mental health facilities, group homes, adult day care centers, and private and public social service agencies. Caseworkers work with individuals, couples, families, and groups. They may also meet with teachers, school guidance counselors, principals, doctors, nurses, or other healthcare professionals.

Depending upon your level of education and experience, there are a variety of roles and settings within which you might choose to work. For example, an individual with a bachelor's or master's degree will have greater responsibilities than someone with an associate's degree or a high school diploma. Higher levels of education often lead to greater professional autonomy, higher salaries, and increased opportunities for advancement.

---

[1]The survey was randomly administered to 2,000 NASW members, with a 78% response rate.

Moreover, states and localities differ considerably in terms of the necessary educational qualifications, certifications, or academic degrees that are required to provide services to individuals or families. In some localities, individuals may need only to possess a high school diploma and relevant experience to perform casework services. These caseworkers are often called social work or human service assistants. In other localities, an individual may need to be licensed or certified by the state or possess a bachelor's or master's degree to provide casework services. These individuals are generally called social workers.

Eligibility Specialists and Social Investigators

Caseworkers employed as eligibility specialists and social investigators work for county social service departments to determine what public assistance or housing programs may be available to assist clients, and whether or not an individual or a family qualifies for these benefits. Examples of public assistance programs include Temporary Assistance for Needy Families (TANF), food stamps, Medicaid, Supplement Social Security Income (SSI), childcare subsidies, and housing allowances. Thus, the eligibility specialist may be responsible for meeting with clients for the initial intake appointment, assessing needs, filling out paperwork, investigating and verifying personal resources, examining records of prior application or receipt of public assistance services, and ensuring that clients receive the benefits or services for which they are eligible.

Just as the eligibility specialist must ensure that individuals and families who meet the requirements for assistance receive benefits, it is equally important that eligibility specialists also ensure that individuals and families do not receive benefits for which they are not eligible. The investigation of eligibility must proceed in a systematic and thorough manner. Although the burden of proof for establishing eligibility and conformity to eligibility rules rests on the individual requesting services, the eligibility specialist must diligently review his or her caseload to be sure that valid information has been obtained.

The eligibility specialist must also be sure to comply with federal, state, and local laws and ensure that no individual or family is discriminated against on the basis of race, religion, sexual orientation, disability, or ethnicity. The eligibility specialist may be also be required to reassess eligibility at a later date and to investigate whether individuals and/or families are meeting current means tests (e.g., income, money in bank, and other assets), work requirements, or other eligibility requirements that determine continuing public assistance services.

Caseworkers who investigate whether or not an individual or family meets the criteria for benefits are often referred to as social investigators. So, for example, social investigators may conduct home visits for the purpose of obtaining and/or conveying additional information, or verifying living arrangements and conditions. In some states or municipalities, eligibility specialists or social investigators may not actually provide casework services to individuals and families, but, rather, refer them to social workers or social work assistants, who provide ancillary services, such as foster home placement or placement of aging adults in nursing homes.

Christy Biaconi, who worked as a housing voucher caseworker in Ithaca, New York, offered the following thoughts about the rewards and also the challenges of assisting clients with housing needs:

> *"I enjoyed the opportunity to work with people directly. To let them know the services that were available. . . . The educational aspect of it. We were helping low-income people get into safe and affordable housing. There was a sense of social justice work being done. It was my first job in human services. We got to meet with people in individual and group settings. We also made referrals to other programs in the area that they might need, and answered questions about how the programs worked. There were people that we could get out of the shelter and into an apartment in under 30 days. Sometimes even less time than that. But we had to operate within the constraints of the program. We were mainly dealing with paperwork. We had an extremely intense caseload, a caseload of over 200. It was enormous. And that was the average caseload. It was enormous. You know how boggling that can be? We couldn't get everything done. That part was frustrating. I had a good supervisor. She helped me to prioritize, to know what was critical. She was very helpful. She was excellent."*

She identified what she thought were important qualities for caseworkers to have:

> *"You have to know how to prioritize. Organization is huge; so much paperwork and case files. Without a good system you can get overwhelmed. You need empathy because it's hard to deal with the influx of cases that are brought day after day after day. You have to realize that you're not responsible for the outcomes. The client has responsibilities there. It took me a while to learn this."*

Christy also identified how she and her supervisor were able to make a significant change in the organization of the agency:

> *"One of the things that happened was we completely restructured the office. We gave up on individual caseloads. We all worked on all of the cases together. We all worked on different aspects of a case. Everyone shared the cases. This reduced the stress for clients. We were able to process more cases."*

Child, Family, and Child Welfare Casework

Child and family social workers and child welfare caseworkers typically work for individual and family services agencies, foster care agencies, diagnostic programs, preventative service programs, group homes, residential treatment facilities, and state or local governments. They may also work in the family court system. These workers may be known as child welfare workers, family services workers, and child protective service workers.

Child, family, and child welfare workers provide social services and professional assistance to help improve the social and psychological functioning of children and their families. They may, for example, provide support to assist single parents, arrange adoptions, or help find foster homes for neglected, abandoned, or abused children. Child and family social workers may also provide therapeutic services to children and adolescents in group homes or residential facilities, as well as work with families in order to maximize the possibility of returning children to their families.

Barb Barry, an MSW-level foster and preventative caseworker for the Department of Social Services in Broome County, New York, described her role as follows:

> "Primarily what we do is provide services for children and families that come into family court. The kids are either in foster care or at risk of being placed in foster care. The court orders provide specific areas that need to be addressed. For example, a parent may be required to receive substance abuse counseling under the order of the court. Part of the job is to hook people up with services . . . a case management sort of thing . . . make sure that service needs that the child has, either at home or in foster care, have been met, for example, education needs or mental health needs. The main purpose is to work on relationships. In foster care, there is a constant monitoring that regular visitations are occurring. If the child is in the home, then we address the relationship between the parent and child in the home. Arrange for counseling, if necessary. . . . A large part of what we do is see people in their environments, in schools, in their homes, at relatives' homes . . . it's about going out to people and working in the environment."

She described what she liked about her role as a foster and preventative caseworker:

> "In casework, there is room for change. Sometimes it's not huge. When you spend significant amounts of time with people in their homes, you pick up subtleties that you might miss otherwise. You see the house is cleaner. They have new rental furniture. The relationship is tied to this. I know all about them. . . . About the neighborhood, schools, Christmas presents, being able to see the changes, smooth things along the way. . . . When people are able to take a case and start seeing progress. When you can return a kid back to their home from services. I think that's really rewarding."

Barb also spoke about the challenges of working in foster and preventative care:

> *"Sometimes there are so many systems to work with within the job. It can get overwhelming . . . foster care workers, substance abuse prevention, mental health prevention, foster parents, social worker of foster parents. Sometimes there are 25–30 people working on a case. It's hard to combine everyone's ideas. The case management piece comes in. It's tricky. . . . You've got to do a bit of work with everybody to keep everyone happy. It's important to be open. . . . to ask people for their input. Sometime it's a matter of getting back to the child welfare mantra, 'Best interest of the child.' Also, we are mandated to provide services in terms of what the court says we have to do."*

Casework with Aging Adults

Due to the large numbers of aging baby boomers, along with advances in healthcare that are extending the average life span, the field of casework with aging adults—gerontology—will be a burgeoning area of specialty for case-workers in the years to come. Gerontology caseworkers offer services for senior citizens; run support groups for family caregivers or for the adult children of aging parents; advise aging adults or family members about housing, transportation, homemaker services, in-home care, meals-on-wheels, senior center programs, medical alert services, advance care directives (i.e., living wills, heathcare proxies, and "do not resuscitate" or DNR directives), adult day care, and long-term care; and coordinate and monitor these services. Other areas of service in gerontology include addressing health and mental health issues of aging adults, elder abuse, advocacy, employment discrimination, palliative or end-of-life care, and protective services for seniors, which monitor whether seniors are at risk for neglect or abuse.

Sally Ryan, who worked as a caseworker in the field of aging for eight years in Tompkins County in New York State, had this to say about working for the Office for the Aging:

> *"Working for the Office for the Aging was very rewarding because the program and staff were dedicated to responding to clients' needs and*

keeping the program flexible enough to individualize care. Clients appreciated the program and I had the time to really listen to my clients. I learned a lot about depression, dementia, heart disease, and a ton of other medical issues. I learned a lot about how I want to be when I am older. It was rewarding to become very skilled at assessing someone's long term care needs and offering support and guidance along the way. I also enjoyed collaborating with other agencies, and working on larger issues facing the elderly. It was fun. Every day was different. It felt very nice to be connecting people up with the right services. Helping them to stay in their homes as long at it was safe."

Sally provided an example of a time that she was able to provide help and make a difference:

"It was interesting because we used to get calls from around the country. A daughter from California once called to talk about things that she was worried about with her mother. So we offered to go and knock on her mother's door, let her know that we were from the Office for the Aging, and describe what services were available for her. When we went to see her, she was very friendly and happy to see me. She said that she wasn't able to get upstairs anymore. She was disoriented. You could tell that she couldn't get out so well anymore. I told her what was available. She didn't want anyone to come into her home. So we worked together. Built trust . . . I was able to hook her up with shopping services, arranged for her to go to the doctor, arranged for a neighbor to take her to church. I felt like I was doing a lot to improve the quality of her life."

Sally also spoke to the qualities that are necessary in order to be a caseworker:

"You need to care about vulnerable people and enjoy your clients. It can be hard emotional work. When a person's in pain or has been treated poorly for a long time, they are not always appreciative. It helps to be someone that looks for strengths in people and in unfriendly work environments, AND it really helps to be organized, have good follow through, and be efficient with paperwork."

Sally summed up her feelings as follows:

> *"Casework is challenging on many levels. In my experience, working with the clients is the easiest and most rewarding part."*

Medical and Public Health Casework

Medical and public health social workers provide individuals, families, or vulnerable populations with the psychosocial support needed to cope with chronic, acute, or terminal illnesses, such as Alzheimer's disease, cancer, or AIDS. They may also advise family caregivers, counsel patients, and help plan for patients' needs after discharge by arranging for at-home services, from meals-on-wheels to oxygen equipment. Some work on interdisciplinary teams that evaluate certain kinds of patients—geriatric or organ transplant patients, for example. Specific areas of service include adult health, acute care, case management, pediatrics, chronic care, advocacy, administration, rehabilitation, public health issues. Medical and public health caseworkers and social workers may work for hospitals, nursing and personal care facilities, individual and family services agencies, or local governments.

Brian Flynn, who worked as an emergency room social worker, described his role as follows:

> *"As emergency room social workers, we pretty much met the psychosocial needs of patients. We worked in a level-two trauma center, which served as the trauma center for the area. Any accidents, gunshot wounds, or other emergencies are going to end in that hospital. We did a lot of grief and loss work—sudden loss, traumatic loss, traumatic injuries. There was lots of crisis work, discharge planning for older folk, like those who lived alone and for whom it wasn't safe to live alone. We assisted anyone who came into the hospital for psychosocial assessment or needed higher levels of care. We also screened for elder abuse, child abuse, domestic violence, mental health assessments, and psychiatric assessments. We worked nights and weekends and were also available to assist with people on other floors. . . ."*

This is what Brian said he liked about the job:

> *"I enjoyed the pace . . . enjoyed the intensity level . . . enjoyed that you never know what to expect. Every day was different. There was a lot of autonomy, which was both good and bad. The nice thing about it was that there was a lot of responsibility, which felt good. I very much enjoyed working with people with that level of need. There was no question that you are being useful, helpful to people who were experiencing that level of emotion at that moment of their lives. . . . I enjoyed the diversity, young and old, race, ethnicity, men and women. There was no discrimination in terms of who was in the hospital."*

Brian identified some of the challenges of working in the emergency room:

> *"The level of emotion was difficult with people who are experiencing traumatic loss. Pediatric deaths were very difficult. I had good supervision, but sometimes you're there by yourself. It teaches you to think on your feet. It would be nice if there were other social workers to consult with. . . . The medical team values the role of the social worker. It was very much an interdisciplinary team approach."*

Brian suggested that some of the following skill sets and qualities are necessary to succeed in the job:

> *"There were a number of situations where you were required to juggle the needs of multiple grieving families. You need to be able to do very quick assessment . . . be there for them in the sense of support at such a horrible time . . . You need to be able to multitask, prioritize, build rapport quickly, do quick assessments. You have to learn to be comfortable with the level of intensity, the pace . . . it's head spinning at times. . . . You need a sense of humor . . . to be thick-skinned; people yell at each other. You need to be comfortable with some of the things you see, the sight of blood, limbs hanging off. You need strength, perseverance. I don't know what drives you, motivates you to come back every day . . . it is incredibly hard, but very rewarding. I wouldn't trade the experience for anything in the world."*

Mental Health and Substance Abuse Casework and Case Management

Mental health and substance abuse caseworkers provide assessment and treatment services to individuals with mental illness or substance abuse problems, including abuse of alcohol, tobacco, or other drugs. Such services include individual and group therapy, outreach, crisis intervention, social rehabilitation, and training in skills of everyday living. They also may help plan for supportive services to ease patients' return to the community. Other areas of service include screening and assessment, counseling, and case management.

Therapy services are usually provided by MSW-level social workers, with training in mental and behavioral health services. Social workers who provide mental health counseling or psychotherapy may be known as clinical or psychiatric social workers. Alcohol treatment is usually provided by caseworkers who are certified alcoholism counselors (CACs). Mental health and substance abuse social workers are often referred to as clinical social workers. They mainly work in hospitals, substance abuse treatment centers, individual and family services agencies, or local.

Ann Dolan works as a supportive case manager for the Mental Hygiene Department in Chenango County, New York. She described her role as follows:

> *"There are three levels to mental health case management. First, there are regular case managers who meet with clients, as needed. Second, there are supportive case managers . . . that's what I do . . . who are required to meet with Medicaid eligible clients twice a month, otherwise the agency won't get paid. Supportive case managers have a caseload of about 20. Third, there are intensive case managers who have to meet with clients four times a month. Their caseload is 12. Supportive case management has their budget paid through the New York Office of Mental Health. . . . People are referred to case management through therapists at the mental health clinic when it is apparent that they don't have the wherewithal, energy, or knowledge to get through the number of agencies that they are required to work with . . . for example, DSS, or Social Security. Maybe they don't have an income. They can't work. They may have medical problems or depression. There*

are all kinds of reasons why clients get referred to case management. They are really looking for something to change. . . . They are ready to begin to do what is necessary to make a change. All I can do is grease the wheels. They still have to drive the vehicle. Maybe they can't drive. . . . It can take years. The average length of working with someone is three years. Some are seen as long as seven years. Short-term clients are the exception."

Ann offered the following observations on what is necessary in order to be successful in this role:

"To do this job, you genuinely have to like people. Some people you'll like more than others. But if you show up thinking that people are trying to get free things, then you're setting yourself up for a miserable career. The clients want a better life for themselves, but they don't have the tools. . . . You genuinely have to like people. Have to see the best in people. You need to have an open heart, an open mind and an open heart. Not be too rigid . . . be flexible, and creative, with limited resources. You also have to be a bit of a salesman . . . need to get on the phone and sell your cause. You need to be kind. You are working with people who are tired and burned out."

As you can see from these narratives, caseworkers perform a great variety of tasks in the service of their roles. The work is challenging and rewarding. Caseworkers must bring important skills and personal qualities to their work in order to be successful. The next chapter will introduce you to some of the basic skills and procedures of casework and social work practice.

CHAPTER two

SKILLS AND PROCEDURES OF CASEWORK

OVERVIEW

Despite the variety of specialized fields and settings within which case-workers are employed; there are certain basic skills and procedures that all helping professionals must master in order to perform their jobs effectively and responsibly. These basic core skills and procedures include understanding how to establish and maintain effective working relationships, knowing how to conduct a successful interview, showing competency in performing an assessment, identifying how and when to make appropriate referrals, having familiarity with proper record-keeping formats, and maintaining a thorough understanding of ethical, legal, and other professional responsibilities. This chapter will acquaint you with some of the basic skills and procedures that are essential for good casework.

INITIAL REQUEST FOR SERVICES

The initial contact that is made by a prospective client to an agency serves as an important source of information for both the client and the agency. First impressions can have an enormous impact and may be key determinants of whether or not a caseworker will be successful in establishing a working relationship or alliance with a client. Sometimes the very first encounter with a client occurs over the telephone, even before the client sets foot in the office. Thus, during the initial phone contact, it will be important for the interviewer to remain pleasant and positive, while obtaining necessary information in a concise and comprehensive manner. The first impression can sometimes make or break the establishment of a successful working relationship.

Agencies will vary in terms of the kinds of questions that will be asked of the client in the initial intake interview and who will ask them. Sometimes an assigned intake worker will routinely screen prospective clients; at other times, a secretary or caseworker may conduct the initial phone screening. Often a form will be filled out, either on paper with black pen, or logged directly into the computer. The intake interviewer will usually ask what the initial request is for and check on basic eligibility requirements. For example, if a potential client is calling a social services agency to inquire about Medicaid benefits, the interviewer will want to know the individual's address to be sure that the office takes care of that geographical location. If an individual is phoning a mental health center, the interviewer will want to know whether the potential client has the proper insurance coverage to be seen by that particular clinic.

In addition to compiling basic demographic information, such as name, address, and phone numbers, the interviewer will want to inquire about the presenting problem or complaint. The interviewer will want to ascertain why the individual is phoning for an appointment and by whom the client was referred. The client may be either self-referred or referred by a third party. For example, older adults may be referred for services by the local

Office for the Aging; children are often referred by a school guidance counselor or family doctor. In the case of a minor, a parent or guardian will usually phone for an appointment.

Another important function of the initial contact with a client is to determine how urgently the client needs to be seen by the agency. For example, if a client is phoning for housing assistance, the interviewer would want to know whether the individual currently has a place to live. If a person is phoning an outpatient mental health clinic for an appointment, the intake interviewer will want to know whether the person is currently suicidal, homicidal, or having psychotic symptoms, such as hallucinations or delusions, to determine whether that individual should be seen in the agency immediately or referred to a hospital, or whether the intake interviewer may need to call 911. Once the initial intake interview is completed, an appointment will be given or a referral made to another agency. If the caller is appropriate for the agency, an appointment is usually given and the client or family comes in for the first interview.

PREPARING FOR THE INITIAL INTERVIEW

To prepare for the initial interview, the worker will want to review the intake information. He or she may wish to note any areas that need further clarification and look for gaps or missing information that can be filled in during the first interview. Additionally, workers may wish to "tune in" (Shulman 2005) to potential areas of difficulty that the client may exhibit during the appointment. For example, if clients have had a number of different workers in the past, the new worker might anticipate that the client may wonder whether the worker will take a genuine interest in the case, or whether the worker is long for the agency. Often, clients will be somewhat nervous at the first appointment. They may not know what to expect, or may not have had good experiences with workers in the past. For some, visiting a caseworker may be embarrassing or perceived as representing a personal failure. Tuning in to these potential client reactions can be a useful tool in preparing for the initial interview.

The worker needs also to tune in to her or his own preconceptions about the client and the kinds of issues the client may be presenting with, in order to better prepare for the interview. The worker may feel hesitant to work with particular clients because of the information contained on the intake form, or may have already developed erroneous ideas about the client that may shape the work in a way that is not helpful to the client. A good rule of thumb is to try to keep an open mind when meeting with a client, so that you are able to base your assessment on what the client is bringing to the interview, not on how someone else has interpreted the client's issues. Often, clients will present very differently with different workers.

For example, a female client with a history of domestic violence may present herself as inhibited and nonverbal with a male worker, but may feel more comfortable and able to open up with a female worker. Also, busy intake workers may leave out important information about the client that may cast the client's situation in a light that does not do justice to the client's predicament.

Workers must also tune in to their own personal feelings when reading intake forms and preparing for the first interview. There may be clients, for example, whose issues are similar to your own, and you may feel prematurely or falsely sure that you will understand the client's needs. On the other hand, you may be planning to work with someone for whom you have already developed an instant dislike, based upon an assumption that the client will behave like someone from your past with whom you did not have an easy relationship. At still other times, you may experience fear or anxiety about meeting a potential client with whom you worry you will not be taken seriously. For example, if a young worker is preparing to meet with an older couple, he or she should tune in to any potential anxiety that may arise about taking on an authority role with individuals who are older, or, if a female worker is scheduled to see a woman who is the victim of domestic violence, the worker may want to tune in to any feelings that she may have about the woman's potential decision to remain with her spouse.

THE WAITING ROOM

Clients' experiences in the waiting room can have a profound impact on how they behave in the first interview. As you, the worker, prepare for the first interview, ask yourself the following questions. How crowded is the waiting room? How respectfully are clients dealt with by the receptionist? How long does the client have to wait in the waiting room? Does the waiting room reflect a diversity of cultures, as exemplified by the racial and ethnic makeup of people depicted on agency brochures or posters on walls? Is a restroom easily accessible? Is there a separate play area for children? Is adequate parking available? All of these kinds of questions can play a dramatic part in the way in which the client behaves in the first interview. Thus, in order to do an adequate and holistic assessment in the first interview, you must be sensitive to the ways in which the client is made to feel either welcome and valued by the agency or unwelcome and devalued. This will also assist you in tuning in to how clients may be feeling as they initially enter your office. Acknowledging any unnecessary wait or other unpleasant aspect of their experiences in the waiting room will be helpful in establishing initial rapport.

THE FIRST INTERVIEW

During the first interview, the caseworker has two main tasks—completing a social history or assessment form, and establishing rapport. The first task requires that the worker obtain sufficient information to begin to develop an assessment of a client's strengths and needs. The first task also requires that the worker and client develop an action plan that identifies objectives and goals and how they will be achieved. The worker, in collaboration with the client, will want to determine not only what the needs of the client are, but also, whether and how the agency can best address those needs. In some cases, the client may need a referral to another agency to address unanticipated needs that arise within the course of the first interview.

The caseworker's second main task during the first interview is to establish rapport. In addition to asking questions and obtaining information pertinent to the client's situation and reason for being there, it will be equally important for the worker to convey that he or she is genuinely interested in helping the client, and is competent enough to accomplish the job. This is an especially important function of the first interview. Thus, it will be important for the worker to be respectful of the client; maintain good eye contact, if culturally appropriate; and be sensitive to the cues of the client.

To establish rapport, the worker needs to be aware of the client's mood and demeanor. This may be accomplished, in part, by observing the client's non-verbal behavior and appearance.

These two tasks—conducting the assessment and establishing rapport—usually go hand in hand. That is, in order to best derive important information from the client, the worker must help the client to feel at ease. This is done through the process of establishing rapport. On the other hand, the best way to establish rapport is to demonstrate to the client that you are competent and interested in helping the client. This is best accomplished through a thorough and effective examination of the client's needs and how the agency may best meet them. Thus an effective assessment cannot take place without establishing rapport, and rapport is best established through the worker's skill in obtaining important information about the client's life.

The Social History

Most agencies will use a specific form to record the social history of the client. Depending on the setting and the kinds of services provided by the agency, the form may be called a social history form, a psychosocial assessment, or the more holistic bio-psychosocial-cultural-spiritual assessment.

While the types of social history forms that are used vary, there is some basic information that is usually required from the client. This information includes a description and history of the presenting problem or issues; important background information about the client's current life and history; the caseworker's impressions and recommendations; and the case disposition.

Description and History of the Presenting Problem

In the first session, the worker will want to find out from the client just what brings him or her to the agency. This will become part of the initial assessment and will be recorded on the social history or other assessment form that the agency may use.

Initially, it will be unlikely that the client will be able to report his or her presenting problem in an organized or comprehensive manner. Often, the client is overwhelmed, and it is precisely for this reason that he or she is seeking help. Clients will likely need help from the worker in terms of prioritizing problems or integrating seemingly disparate or unrelated problems into a coherent narrative. Part of the job of the worker in the first session will be to identify, in collaboration with the client, what the presenting problem is and how to characterize it accurately within a phrase or two that can be recorded in the presenting problem section of the assessment form. (See "Skills Used in the First Interview," p. 33, for an in-depth discussion of how to distill the presenting problem from the client's initial narrative.)

In constructing the presenting problem statement, you want to provide answers to the five "w" questions—who, what, when, where, and why—that are commonly taught to prospective journalists when they are learning how to craft the opening sentence of a newspaper article. Also, it is often helpful to provide information pertaining to how the client came to be seen in the agency. For example, was the client self-referred, or was she referred by another agency, or a family member? You will also want to include pertinent identifying information, such as the age of the client and his or her marital status.

Examples of presenting problem statements might include the following:

> "Ms. D. is a single 27-year-old, African American, self-referred woman who came to the agency today complaining of depressive symptoms, including tearfulness, loss of appetite, and difficulty sleeping, following the breakup of an intimate relationship with her boyfriend of three years."

> "Mrs. K. is a 52-year-old, Latina, divorced mother of three grown children who came to the clinic today due to difficulties coping with her live-in mother's deteriorating health. She was referred by her primary doctor."

> "Joey, a nine-year-old Caucasian boy from an intact family of four, was referred to the clinic today by his guidance counselor due to her concerns about his increasingly aggressive behavior in school."

In addition to the presenting statement or statements, you will also want to include information pertaining to the history of the presenting problem.

For example, you will want to find out whether the client has experienced this kind of problem before, and, if so, how many times; the severity of the problem; and whether or not the client has received services for this problem in the past. You should state the nature of these services and note also whether the client perceived prior services to be helpful or not. The history of the presenting problem should be recorded within no more than a single paragraph.

Paragraphs summarizing the history of the presenting problem might resemble the following:

> Ms. D. reports a protracted history of recurrent episodes of moderate depression beginning at age 16. All of these episodes occurred following the loss of an important relationship. For example, at age 16, Ms. D.'s best friend moved out of town. She reports that she was inconsolable and unable to get out of bed for two weeks. On another occasion, when she was 18, she became despondent following a breakup with her boyfriend. She was unable to eat or sleep and reports that she lost 10 pounds in one week. She further reports that although she feels acutely sad during these episodes, the primary symptoms of tearfulness and sleep disturbance typically subside within a period of approximately four weeks. She has sought professional help from a therapist on two prior occasions. She found both of these experiences to be helpful. She felt that she benefited from having someone to talk to.

> Mrs. K. explains that her mother came to live with her two years ago, after her youngest child graduated from college and moved across the country. She reports that she was hesitant, at first, to let her mother move in, due to the fact that the two women have historically had a conflicted relationship. She describes her mother as critical; she is always harping at Mrs. K. about her housecleaning habits. Her mother was recently diagnosed with Alzheimer's disease. Additionally, her mother has arthritis, which makes it difficult for her to ambulate without the assistance of a walker. Mrs. K. reports that she has been trying to encourage her mother to move into an assisted living facility, but her mother re-

fuses to go, stating that she wishes to live with her daughter. Mrs. K. feels guilty about wanting her mother to move out, but is finding that she can no longer care for her mother without professional help. This is Mrs. K.'s first time seeking professional services.

The guidance counselor reports that Joey has been throwing erasers at the other children, talking back to his teacher, and refusing to participate in recess. She further states that Joey's school-related behavior problems began approximately two months ago and have become increasingly worse over the last two weeks. Joey's mother, who accompanied him to the appointment today, states that Joey has never before had behavior problems in school, and has not been exhibiting any behavioral difficulties at home. She did report, however, that she recently gave birth to her second child, a son, two months ago.

Background Information

In addition to stating the presenting problem and providing information about the background or history of the presenting problem, a very important part of the social or psychosocial history is to examine the background and contexts of an individual's life. Contextual factors can serve to enhance or diminish one's adaptation to environmental stressors. The objective of examining context is to create a broad understanding of an individual and his or her functioning in various areas. Thus the assessment also provides information about where to intervene in the individual's life to best provide support.

In order to assess an individual's current functioning within a holistic context, the worker must take into account a number of factors, including biological, psychological, social, and spiritual factors. These factors should be included as part of the background information.

Biological Factors
This includes information relevant to the client's health, for example, date of last complete physical, current medical conditions, medical history, nutrition,

exercise, sleep, and any substance use. Biological information also includes any medications that the client may currently be taking, or has taken in the past. In a psychiatric setting, caseworkers should note any history of mental illness in the family, and include a current mental status report. You should also identify any barriers to receiving healthcare services that the client may be experiencing, such as lack of insurance, inadequate childcare help, or transportation issues.

Psychological Factors

All psychological signs and/or symptoms that the client may have should also be recorded in the assessment. A sign is any observable indication of the client's difficulty; a symptom is how the client perceives or reports his or her condition. The psychological assessment should also include results of psychological testing, if applicable; areas of adaptation or vulnerability; and coping mechanisms. The history of a presenting psychological problem or complaint should also be noted, along with any previous treatment of a given condition. Areas of strength, such as intelligence, insight, social skills, and any other special talents, should also be highlighted and included as part of the assessment.

Social Factors

Any pertinent social aspects of the client's current life and past history should be included in the assessment. Current social information might include, for example, a description of the family, household, and other significant relationships. Also included should be social supports, including friends, neighbors, extended family, or memberships in clubs, or the lack thereof, if applicable.

Another important area to include is the client's financial situation, and any financial hardships that the client may be experiencing. You may also note sources of income, whether they are from a job, or Social Security disability, or another source. Additionally, you will include a description of the client's current housing situation, including the physical layout of their home and whether there is adequate space for household members (e.g., how many bedrooms, bathrooms, etc.).

Other areas to include are any significant life stressors, such as major life changes, phase of life issues, or losses. Important past social history might include history of marital or intimate relationships, and dating history. Educational history, employment history, military history, and any legal history or history of incarcerations will also be included in this section.

Spiritual Factors

Spirituality may be defined as "the human search for transcendence, meaning, and connectedness beyond the self" (Sherwood 1998, 80). Increasingly, the role of spirituality has been found to be a significant factor in working with a range of clients and in support of the issues for which clients seek casework services. For example, spirituality has been found to be significant for older adults, including elders in long-term care such as nursing homes, as well as African Americans, Muslims, Christians, individuals with chronic mental health issues, people in addiction recovery, and those with health issues and serious illnesses.

Thus, it is important that the initial assessment should include aspects of a person's spirituality or religion. For example, if a person's church is important to him and he has recently moved, he may be experiencing the loss of his church community and important relationships within that community. This loss can provide additional stress in a person's life.

Several assessment tools may be used in determining the role of spirituality or religion in a client's life. These tools include taking an individual's spiritual history, and the use of spiritual life maps, spiritual genograms, and spiritual eco-maps.

SKILLS USED IN THE FIRST INTERVIEW

According to Shulman (2006, 77), a worker should use five basic skills to help clients manage their presenting problems in the first and subsequent sessions: clarifying the worker's purpose and role; reaching for the client's feedback, partializing the client's concerns, supporting clients in taboo areas, and dealing with issues of authority.

Within the first opening minutes of the first interview, the worker can help to lessen the client's potential anxiety by explaining what it is that he or she is doing—the worker's purpose and role. This is a way of dealing directly with the client's anxiety. So, for example, the worker may begin by providing a brief introduction of him- or herself, a brief description of the kinds of services offered by the agency, and an identification of some of the ways that the worker may be able to help the client. Hopefully, this will ease some of the client's apprehensiveness about what to expect during the course of the first interview.

Second, the worker will want to answer any initial questions that the client may have. The client, for example, may want to know the worker's credentials or where the worker obtained his or her education. These questions should be answered with as little defensiveness as possible. Allowing and inviting clients to share their apprehensions and worries about the beginning working relationship will help to lay the foundation for the building of trust in the relationship. Empathy, warmth, and genuineness continue to be the best predictors of successful outcomes in casework. If the worker incorporates these characteristics throughout the first interview, there is a fairly good chance that a good rapport between worker and client will be established.

Personal questions, such as how old the worker is or whether the worker has children, do not need to be answered. Instead, the worker may wish to direct the client back to a consideration of what brings him or her to the appointment. The worker may also try to identify whether there may be some initial worries or concerns that may underlie personal questions. For example, the worker may respond to questions about experience or age by asking whether the client may have some concerns as to whether the worker will be competent or capable of assisting the client in the resolution of difficulties. The client might then respond that she hasn't had good experiences with helpers in the past.

The most important question for the worker to ask will be to find out the reason for the appointment, or the presenting problem. After referring to the initial intake form to verify the initial request, the worker may choose to ask a more open-ended question, such as "How can I be of help to you today?" The decision as to whether the worker will begin with an open-ended question, one that invites the client to provide a narrative of the presenting problem, or a more closed-ended question, one that requires a yes, no, or other short answer, will depend on a number of factors. For example, if the worker is interested in the client's expanding upon the presenting problem, the worker would be likely to ask an open-ended question to obtain additional information. On the other hand, if a client appears to be overwhelmed by a number of complaints or problems, the worker might wish to help contain the client by asking more directive and closed-ended questions to start.

Examples of open-ended questions might include the following:

▶ What brings you here today?
▶ How can I be of assistance to you today?
▶ How have you handled this situation in the past?
▶ Can you describe a time when you were successful in managing this issue?

Examples of closed-ended questions might include the following:

▶ Where did you grow up?
▶ How many hours of sleep did you get last night?
▶ What kinds of medications are you taking?
▶ How many children do you have?

In addition to the presenting problems or complaints, the worker will want to find out the history of the presenting problem (when the problem first manifested itself) and why the client has chosen to seek help at this time. The worker will also want to identify any precipitants to the presenting problem; that is, whether there was an event that preceded the first manifestation of the problem.

For example, a worker interviewing a depressed patient in an outpatient mental health clinic would want to identify if the symptoms of depression followed the breakup of a relationship, or if they appeared to come out of the blue. By obtaining detailed information about the problem and its potential causes, this worker will be in a better position to assess the nature of the depression and identify a plan of action.

In addition to identifying the presenting problem and its history, the worker will also obtain background information about the client's life. For example, the worker will want to find out about the client's family of origin, birth and childhood history, educational history, significant relationships, marriages, education, medical history, legal history, and military service.

During the course of the initial interview, the worker will perform an assessment of the client's strengths, which includes identifying support systems, internal and external resources, coping abilities, and wishes/dreams for the future. The worker will also identify potential areas of vulnerability or stress, such as lack of social or familial supports, strained financial resources, feelings of hopelessness or depression, or a pattern of unhealthy or dysfunctional relationships.

Often, clients will identify a number of problems that are of concern to them. In these cases, the worker must help the client to partialize or prioritize the problems and issues, so that they may be more manageable for both the worker and the client. The client should be included in the process of partialization, or determining which problems will be addressed first.

The client may also need assistance in addressing issues that are potentially taboo or embarrassing. For example, clients sometimes need to talk about subjects that aren't usually discussed in polite conversation, such as money concerns, relationship or sexual problems, issues with anger management, substance abuse problems, or depression. The worker needs to be tuned in to the sensitive nature of some of the client's concerns, and find ways to facilitate conversations about them. A worker might accomplish this by identifying the specific area of taboo and labeling it as such. For example, the worker might say, "I wonder if it might be hard to speak about your gambling problem. I don't suppose it's the first thing that comes up in everyday conversation." The worker may also express empathy for the client by stating, "I can understand that it may be hard for you to talk about the sexual difficulties that you are experiencing with your wife."

Caseworkers also need to be aware that clients will likely view them as authority figures. Because many individuals have characteristically been socialized to suppress their real and sometimes negative feelings toward authority figures, a worker should promote an environment that invites the expression of negative feedback and allows a client to put angry feelings into words. This will help to prevent clients from later acting out their resentment toward the worker, as might be reflected in missing appointments or coming in late, and will also provide some practice in learning how to express anger in words, rather than simply discharging it through action. Thus, a worker might mention in an initial appointment that he or she will invariably misunderstand the client at times, and would like to encourage the client to express feelings of dissatisfaction when they arise.

CONTRACTING

The initial interview serves several important functions. In addition to obtaining and clarifying information, the worker will begin to establish a working contract with the client. This contract doesn't need to be written; it may be a verbal agreement between the worker and client specifying the mutual tasks of both the agency and the client. Schwartz (1971) characterized the concept of contracting as including both clients' needs and also the mission of the agency. Finding a way to meet the clients' needs within the parameters of the services provided by the agency is what constitutes a contract. Schwartz (1971, 8) described it as follows:

> "The convergence of these two sets of tasks—those of the clients and those of the agency—creates the terms of the contract that is made between the client group and the agency. This contract, openly reflecting both stakes, provides the frame of reference for the work that follows, and for understanding when the work is in process, when it is being evaded and when it is finished."

By the conclusion of the first session, the worker should have a good sense of what is bringing the client to the agency and whether or not there is a good fit among the worker, the client, and the agency. Equally as important, the client should have a good sense of how he or she will work with the agency to achieve mutually agreed-upon goals.

Shulman (2005) makes the important point that the contract provides a structure that is designed, in part, to bring focus and a sense of safety to the client, who is coming into the agency for help. Moreover, the contract should be understood as a process that is malleable and open to change and modification over time, as the client's needs shift and become better understood by both parties.

Contracting Skills with Mandated Clients

A particularly challenging contracting process can be experienced when working with mandated clients. These are clients that are involuntary and are coming for help because they have been told they have to by a third party. For example, individuals are sometimes mandated for services by the court system, such as when individuals are told that they must seek treatment for alcoholism or face jail time. Other examples of mandated clients include employees who are referred by their Employee Assistance Program (EAP) offices, or parents who are referred by family court to receive counseling before they may be allowed to regain custody of their children. Although some of these individuals are highly motivated for help despite their involuntary status, other mandated clients may be ambivalent or highly resistant to receiving services. These latter clients pose particular challenges for workers in the contracting phase.

Workers must be ready to openly discuss obstacles to the development of a working relationship. While the same skills required of workers with all clients in the first session will be necessary in negotiating a contract with mandated clients, workers must employ empathy for the client's involuntary status and a search for common ground, while still maintaining a demand that the client work to achieve mutually agreed-upon treatment goals. Thus, skills utilized with mandated clients include, among others, the worker exploring his or her own feelings about working with a potentially resistant client, and the use of an empathic demand for work (Shulman 2005).

RAPPORT

As indicated earlier, warmth, empathy, and genuineness, also referred to as WEG, are essential ingredients in the development of a positive rapport between worker and client. WEG has also been found to be a salient predictor of successful treatment outcomes.

Warmth on the part of a worker includes such attitudes as being nonjudgmental, open, respectful, receptive, and friendly. Friendliness, by the way, is not the same as being a friend to a client. A worker provides services to clients on behalf of an agency. Workers are expected to maintain professional boundaries with clients; becoming friends transcends professional boundaries. Friendliness reflects an interest in the client's well-being, and a wish to be of help. Warmth refers to emotional presence and making oneself available for emotional connection and attunement.

Empathy refers to the ability to put yourself in the shoes of another, while still maintaining your perspective as a separate person. Empathy may be reflected through an ability to put the unexpressed feelings of a client into words, or simply by providing support to clients who are going through trying and difficult life situations.

Genuineness simply refers to being yourself within the boundaries of your role. Clients often respond better to individuals who are down to earth and not putting on professional airs to impress or dominate. Making false promises about your ability to help clients does not convey genuineness.

Encouragement is another basic skill that is helpful in establishing rapport with clients. Encouragement may be reflected in such basic casework skills as approaching issues from the client's perspective, identifying client strengths, providing hopefulness for the client, and appreciating the efforts that clients make toward change, whether successful or not.

Encouragement versus Discouragement[1]

Encouragement	Discouragement
The Encourager:	The Discourager:
Says you can	Says you can't
Helps clients to do their best	Wants clients to compete
Helps clients to look for the best in life	Tells clients life is unfair
Believes others are capable	Believes he or she is more capable than the person being helped
Talks directly to people	Talks down to people
Is supportive of others	Is critical of others
Is enthusiastic about others	Is reluctant and wary of others
Is interested in the smallest of accomplishments	Is interested in the smallest of mistakes
Helps clients set realistic expectations	Has unrealistic expectations for clients and gives up easily
Sees resources and strengths in clients	Sees mainly weaknesses and incompetence in clients
Lets clients develop their own personal standards	Sets personal standards for clients
Believes people can improve	Believes people never change

[1]Source: Based on D. Dinkmoyer and L.E. Losoncy, *The Encouragement Book: Becoming a Positive Person* (Englewood Cliffs, NJ: Prentice-Hall, 1980; from Summers 2006).

Othmer and Othmer (1994, 13) identify several additional skills that workers may use to help develop rapport with clients in the first interview and beyond. Although they refer specifically to mental health interviews, these skills may be generalized to other practice settings, as well. These skills include putting the client and yourself at ease, showing compassion, becoming an ally, demonstrating expertise, establishing leadership, and balancing the roles between worker and client in the helping relationship.

Putting the Client and Yourself at Ease

Both worker and client may be nervous and apprehensive at the beginning of their first encounter. In order to help set the stage for a productive first encounter, the worker may need to help the client overcome his or her initial anxiety. This may be accomplished, in part, by the worker first assessing his or her feelings prior to the first meeting. By becoming aware of his or her own feelings toward a client prior to the first encounter, the worker may be better able to direct energy and focus on the client during the session and thus be enabled to demonstrate empathy toward the client's feelings and concerns. Another way that the worker may try to alleviate the potential apprehension of the client may be to engage in small talk at the very beginning of the appointment. Such questions as "Did you have any trouble finding the office?" or "Did you have any trouble finding parking?" may help to put the client at ease.

Nonverbal Signs

The worker should also pay attention to nonverbal signs and cues that the client may be demonstrating, and then respond, appropriately, to those. Types of signs may include territorial, behavioral, and emotional (Othmer & Othmer 1994). Territorial signs include such things as where the client chooses to sit in the consulting room. If the client takes the chair closest to you, that might be a sign that the client is more comfortable with dependency. If the client moves the chair very close to you, this might indicate unmet dependency needs. Of course, it could also indicate that the client is hard of hearing. If, on the other hand, a client moves the chair further away from you, then the client may be displaying some anxiety or fear of intimacy or closeness. Initially, it may be best to respect the cues that are communicated through the signs and behave accordingly, unless you feel inordinately intruded upon by doing so, or the client has moved the chair to the absolute opposite end of the room or out into the hallway, behavior that you may need to comment upon in order to function effectively. Otherwise, as the work progresses and you have developed beginning rapport with the client, you may choose to comment on territorial signs in order to increase insight.

Behavioral signs may include avoiding eye contact, fidgeting, yawning, or moving furniture around. Sometimes it can be useful to try to put the behavioral communication into words. For example, the caseworker might reflect on how difficult it can be to talk about painful or embarrassing topics, or wonder aloud in a playful manner whether yawning might be an indication of discomfort with speaking aloud about specific topics.

Emotional signs provide cues as to how the client is feeling, and include the client's facial expression, outward mood, posture, and demeanor. The worker may choose to respond to emotional signs through mirroring facial expressions that express empathy and concern.

Showing Compassion

Another important skill that may be used in the service of establishing rapport is to find out where in the client's life he or she is experiencing distress and conveying compassion. Showing compassion can be expressed through the skill of putting the client's feelings into words, or clarifying whether the worker understands the nature of the client's distress. The worker can also ask the client to speak about the suffering that he or she has experienced

In addition to helping the client learn how to express painful emotions through language and begin the important process of grieving, the client will also then have the experience of being listened to and understood, which can comprise an important healing process in the work. Thus, for example, a worker might say to a recently bereaved widower, "I can imagine that this news was a real blow to you," or "I can see that this loss has been tremendously painful for you." If working with a single mother who has recently lost her job, a worker might say, "I can see why you would be overwhelmed and frightened about how you will be able to take care of yourself and your children."

CULTURAL SENSITIVITY AND AWARENESS

An increasingly important aspect of establishing and maintaining effective helping relationships with clients of all ages concerns the degree to which caseworkers understand their own culture and the cultures of those with whom they work. Unfamiliarity with diverse cultures may cause professionals to misinterpret what they perceive and mistakenly lead them to construct inappropriate diagnoses. For example, Sands (2001) provides the example of African Americans being overdiagnosed with paranoia, when cultural paranoia may be a very adaptive response within a particular cultural/environmental context. Lum (2005, 4) defines cultural competence as "the mastery of a particular set of knowledge, skills, policies, and programs used by the social worker that address the cultural needs of individuals, families, groups, and communities."

In order for caseworkers to effectively serve the needs of an increasingly culturally diverse population, it is necessary for them to incorporate skills of cultural awareness and sensitivity into casework practice. Indeed, many of the clients served by caseworkers are members of groups that are outside of the mainstream culture. There is a vast overrepresentation of children of color, for example, in the child welfare and juvenile justice systems. Healthcare disparities abound, and people of color disproportionately live beneath the poverty line. Perhaps it is because of mainstream culture's impact on diverse individuals and groups that they increasingly find themselves in need of human and social services. In the preface to a popular book on cultural competence that is widely used in social work programs across the country, Terry Cross describes cultural competence very eloquently:

> "Cultural competence looks at clinical issues as being clinical/cultural issues in which behavior cannot be understood outside of the context of culture. Depression cannot be understood outside the context of intergenerational trauma. Parenting cannot be understood outside the legacy of boarding schools or slavery. Self-esteem cannot be understood outside the context of male dominance. Healing cannot be understood outside of the context of spiritual beliefs" (Cross 2003, vii).

To become culturally competent, workers must make culture a focus of all casework practice. Clients' help-seeking behavior, problem-solving strategies, and beliefs about spirituality and healing are all determined by culture. Likewise, culture affects the underlying beliefs, attitudes, and values of all caseworkers. Caseworkers need to find strategies to make visible the cultural lenses through which we all view and understand the world.

According to Weaver (1999), cultural competence consists of three important areas:

- ▶ knowledge about various cultural groups, as well as the recognition that diversity exists within cultural groups
- ▶ skills in working with various cultural groups
- ▶ awareness of one's values, assumptions, and biases. For example, in American culture, there is an emphasis on individuality and personal responsibility. Other cultures, such as Latino or Asian, place an emphasis on community and responsibility to others.

Caseworkers should strive to put aside cultural biases in favor of professional values, including the valuing of diversity and understanding dynamics of difference.

Skills of Cultural Competence

Lum (2003), in referencing Kadushin and Kadushin (1997), suggests several principles that caseworkers need to follow in order to conduct a culturally competent interview with individuals and families from diverse backgrounds:

- ▶ Be aware of cultural factors that may intrude upon the session.
- ▶ Acknowledge stereotypical ideas they hold with reference to the particular group or individual.
- ▶ Apply stereotypes flexibly with a conscious effort to discard the generalization if it does not conform to the particular interviewee.
- ▶ Learn about the culture of the client so as to better understand and contextualize the particular behaviors of an interviewee.
- ▶ Respond to interviewees with respect, empathy, and acceptance, whatever their differences (Lum 2001, 76; Kadushin & Kadushin 1997, 343–344).

SKILLS OF EFFECTIVE COMMUNICATION

In order to establish and maintain a good working relationship with clients, it is necessary for caseworkers to learn skills of effective communication. In addition to learning skills that facilitate communication, workers must also learn how to avoid barriers to good communication. Developing and maintaining good rapport with clients requires being sensitive and thoughtful, both when asking questions and also when responding to a client's questions.

Barriers to Good Communication

Gordon (1975) identified 12 barriers to effective communication. These barriers include:

1. Ordering, directing, commanding—this can serve to eliminate any possible discussion or collaboration between worker and client.

   "You must leave that abusive husband of yours."

   "You should sue him for every penny he's got."

2. Warning, admonishing, threatening—this doesn't allow for an exploration of potential client resistance, and, in fact, is likely to increase it.

   "You'd better bring the right forms in next time."

   "If you don't look for a job next week, you'll be cut off from unemployment."

3. Exhorting, moralizing, preaching—this can make the client feel insignificant or inferior to the worker.

   "A good person wouldn't treat their children that way."

   "If you could just practice some willpower, you'd be able to lose weight."

   "You shouldn't feel that way!"

4. Advising or giving solutions or suggestions—this doesn't allow for input from the client and may serve to allay the worker's impatience.

> *"Just tell him to cut it out."*
>
> *"Stop moping."*
>
> *"Just go in there and tell him you want your money."*

5. Lecturing, teaching, giving logical arguments—this approach similarly doesn't allow for any input from the client, so that you eliminate the possibility of understanding any reluctance on the client's part to follow through.

> *"You just need to decide whether you want to stay in this relationship."*
>
> *"If you get a job, you will have the money to pay your bills."*

6. Judging, criticizing, disagreeing, blaming—this can leave the client feeling demoralized and lessen the client's sense of hope.

> *"It is wrong of you to think like that."*
>
> *"You shouldn't have said that to her."*
>
> *"You don't really feel that way."*
>
> *"It is your fault that happened."*

7. Praising, agreeing—this may be used to keep the worker from exploring painful topics.

> *"You said exactly the right thing."*
>
> *"Everything you do works out well."*

8. Name-calling, ridiculing, shaming—this serves only to make the client feel foolish.

> *"How foolish of you to have done that."*
>
> *"Even your daughter could have handled that better."*
>
> *"You always say the wrong thing."*

9. Interpreting, analyzing, diagnosing—this attributes motivations to the client that may not be true.

> *"The only reason you say that is because you're jealous of her."*
>
> *"You want to keep him dependent on you."*
>
> *"You don't really want to get a job."*

10. Reassuring, sympathizing, consoling, supporting—this cuts the client off from expressing feelings or concerns.

> *"I know it will all work out."*
>
> *"Things are bound to get better."*
>
> *"He'll come around, you'll see."*

11. Probing, questioning, interrogating—can be experienced by clients as prying and can shut down fruitful dialogue.

> *"Why did you go there?"*
>
> *"What were you thinking?"*

12. Withdrawing, distracting, humoring, diverting—this avoids focus on the important issues at hand.

> *"Did you catch the Emmys last night?"*
>
> *"Do you hear that siren?"*
>
> *"Maybe you'll win the lottery."*
>
> *"Maybe you shouldn't think about that."*

Skills of Effective Listening and Responding

In addition to knowing what not to say, there are a number of important ways to effectively listen and respond to clients. These skills include reflective listening, responding to feelings, responding to content, showing appreciation to the client, disarming anger, affirming and challenging clients, and engaging clients collaboratively.

Reflective Listening

One of the most important skills in effective casework is being a good listener. A good listener does not simply sit and receive passively the words of others; a good listener is an active participant in the communication process. A good listener pays attention to the client's facial expressions, tone of voice, behavioral cues, mood, and choice of words. Through reflective listening, you can convey understanding, correct possible misunderstandings, and empathically respond to the feelings and thoughts of your clients.

In fact, current studies in brain research are demonstrating a causal link between the healthy development of the mind and emotional attunement in interpersonal relationships. Studies have demonstrated that empathically attuned responses of caregivers to children contribute to the integration of the left and right brain hemispheres and promote the development of self-soothing. Likewise, emotionally attuned casework relationships facilitate the development of interpersonal safety and trust, and lead to more open and constructive relationships with clients.

Responding to Feelings

Summers (2006) identified two simple steps that caseworkers can use to respond to clients' feelings:

1. Identifying the feeling, whether spoken or nonspoken.
2. Constructing a single statement that specifically includes the feeling.

Examples of empathic responses:

> CLIENT: *"I wasn't able to sleep last night, thinking about my unpaid bills."*
>
> WORKER: *"It's not easy to rest, when you're feeling so worried."*
>
> CLIENT: *"I'm afraid that I won't be able to keep my apartment or feed my kids."*
>
> WORKER: *"It must feel overwhelming to be a single parent."*

Examples of nonempathic responses:

"You'd better call the bill collectors and work out a repayment plan."

"That's what happens when you don't budget your money properly."

Reflective listening also entails paying close attention to a client's reaction to your comments. Clients will usually let you know, either verbally or nonverbally, whether your responses have been helpful or not. Pay attention to whether your comment has facilitated a deeper level of discussion, or whether the flow of communication has suddenly shut down. You can always revisit an earlier comment to repair disconnects and keep the channels of communication open.

For example:

"I noticed that you stopped talking after my last comment. Was it something that I said?"

"You've suddenly become silent. Can you tell me what you're thinking or feeling right now?"

Asking Questions

Caseworkers are required to ask clients questions in order to complete intake material, obtain additional or new information, or clarify something that the client has said. Questions can also be used to encourage ongoing exploration of issues and elaboration of ideas or strategies for change. When asking clients questions, it is useful to avoid framing questions in a way that may be confusing, or shut down communication. The following cautions, offered by Summers (2006), might serve as a helpful guide as to what not to do.

Ask one question at a time. Multiple questions can feel overwhelming to a client and may prevent a clear and focused discussion of an issue. Moreover, a client can feel confused, or as if the worker is impatient or not really interested in what the client has to say.

Avoid sudden changes of subject. This can be disruptive to a client's discourse and can prevent a deeper exploration of material.

Be aware that there are often several answers to any one question. Don't act as though only you know the right answers, or as if you expect the client to respond in a particular way.

Don't make assumptions about a client. Take the time to find out what the client is thinking and feeling.

Be respectful of a client's point of view. Don't try to talk a client out of a particular feeling, or impose your interpretation on a given situation.

Dealing with Silences

Sometimes it is useful for a worker to allow for periods of silence in an interview. This can provide time and space for clients to reflect upon their feelings and thoughts before speaking. At other times, however, periods of silence may mean that a worker's intervention has fallen short or missed its mark; or maybe the client is angry at the worker and unable to say so. At still other times, a client may need assistance in bringing up painful feelings or difficult topics for discussion. Because periods of silence can reflect a potential range of meanings for the client, it is important for the worker to try to discern what the silence may mean.

One of the best tools available to the worker may be to reflect upon his or her own feelings and upon what has just transpired in the session prior to the moment of silence. Did the silence follow an empathic intervention on the part of the worker, or did it seemingly come out of nowhere? It is also important for the worker to explore the meaning of the silence, particularly if the silence has transpired for more than a few minutes.

The worker should be prepared to explore negative feedback. The ability of the worker to nondefensively tolerate the client's negative feedback can allow for the possibility of repairing misunderstandings or lapses in empathy, and provide the building blocks necessary to the development of a trusting relationship, where both participants can begin to take risks in achieving a deeper and more meaningful level of exploration and discussion.

Confrontation

Although the natural inclination of many in polite society is to avoid confrontation at all costs, there are times when a worker must use methods of confrontation to bring out in the open behaviors or ideas that may be potentially destructive to the client, the working relationship, or the worker. For example, any behavior on the part of the client that violates the law or presents an eminent danger to self or others must be confronted immediately.

Confrontation may also be useful when dealing with obstacles to change, especially if clients are unaware of how they may be potentially creating barriers to their own successful problem resolution. At other times, clients may be ambivalent about issues or resolution of difficulties. For example, a father may express a wish to develop a closer relationship with his son, but may avoid opportunities to spend quality time with his son; or an unemployed mother may express a desire to find a job, yet consistently misses scheduled job interviews. The point of confrontation is to bring conflictual issues out in the open in order to facilitate discussion, exploration, and insight into potential problem areas.

Summers (2006, 178–179) offers the following cautions in the use of confrontation:

- ▶ Be matter of fact.
- ▶ Be tentative.
- ▶ Focus on tangible behavior or communication.
- ▶ Take full responsibility for your observations.
- ▶ Be collaborative.
- ▶ Do not accuse.
- ▶ Do not confront because you are angry.
- ▶ Do not be judgmental.
- ▶ Do not give the client a solution.

In order to be successful when using confrontational techniques, it is important to remember some basic rules. If you want someone to consider your point of view, you need to formulate your comments in such a way that they can be heard by the other person. Thus, you must present your question or statement in a way that invites the other person to share his or her observation or feelings. Remember to phrase your comments thoughtfully and show respect for your client. If both worker and client can work together to better understand obstacles or barriers to change, there is a better chance of overcoming them.

Examples of confronting clients may include the following:

> *"You say you are not angry at your wife. Yet, when you speak about the things that she says to you, I find myself feeling annoyed at her. Do you think she may be irritating you more than you think?"*

"I notice that you have a pattern of coming in late for your appointments. Do you think you might be expressing something through this behavior, rather than speaking about it directly with me?"

"Can we both take a look at this and try to understand what might be going on?"

Dealing with Anger

As mentioned earlier, it is important for caseworkers to be able to both solicit and tolerate negative feedback from clients. Sometimes this negative feedback concerns the client's anger. Clients can get angry for a number of reasons. Sometimes a client may feel anger or frustration toward the worker or agency; sometimes a client is overwhelmed or tired, or simply in need of attention or support. Learning how to accept the client's anger appropriately can go a long way toward building a safe and trusting relationship, and can also provide valuable modeling for clients who may have difficulty expressing their anger constructively.

One of the biggest mistakes a worker can make is to take the client's anger personally. A worker who takes the client's anger personally is at risk of becoming defensive or sarcastic; acting as though he or she is in a superior position to the client, or asking a series of rapid-fire questions that may serve to allay the worker's discomfort rather than elicit pertinent information from the client. Responses such as these serve only to fuel the client's anger and frustration, and do little to maintain the working relationship. Instead, anger can be interpreted as a sign that the client's needs are not being met adequately. The worker needs to remain calm and try to identify the concerns that underlie the client's anger.

Moreover, by responding appropriately to a client's anger, you can potentially disarm it. For example, you might be able to identify and understand important feelings that a client has been harboring and thus develop a more empathic view of the client's feelings and struggles. Burns (1980) suggests four steps that workers can take to disarm a client's anger. These steps include 1) expressing appreciation to the client for sharing the feeling; 2) asking for additional information; 3) finding areas of agreement; and 4) beginning to find a solution. To the extent that the anger is not taken personally, you will be better able to disarm the anger and move forward in deepening the relationship and furthering the work (Summers 2006).

Due to the increasing prevalence of violence in our society, caseworkers may increasingly be required to acquire specialized skills in anger management. Indeed, for some clients, an inability to manage their anger may be the centerpiece of their presenting problems. Potter-Efron and Potter-Efron (2006), who have written extensively in the area of anger management, have identified 11 different styles of anger, clustered into three main groups: masked, explosive, and chronic. Masked anger includes anger avoidance, sneaky anger, and anger turned inward. Explosive anger includes sudden, shame-based, deliberate, and excitatory anger. The chronic styles include habitual hostility, paranoia (fear-based anger), moral anger, and resentment/hate. Workers who are not proficient in the area of anger management may refer clients with anger management issues to specialists who are trained to treat these issues.

BARRIERS TO CHANGE

Hepworth et al. (2006) identify several barriers to client change and growth. These barriers include under and over-involvement of worker, cross-racial and cross-cultural barriers, difficulties in establishing trust, and transference and countertransference reactions. They also identify ways that a worker can overcome barriers to client change.

Under-Involvement of Worker

Workers who are burned out or are having difficulty in their own personal lives may have difficulty being there for their clients. Such unavailability may be expressed by lack of empathy, inattentiveness, difficulty remembering the client or the client's story, lethargy, chronic lateness, or canceling of sessions. These behaviors, if consistent and not addressed in a worker's supervision, may cause irreparable barriers to a successful working relationship.

Workers may also develop "compassion fatigue," and must find ways to incorporate self-care into their daily routines. Compassion fatigue occurs when workers consistently put the needs of their clients over the needs of themselves, to the detriment of both parties. One speaker on compassion fatigue provided the story of the worker who happened upon a man in the forest who was trapped beneath a heavy tree limb and beseeched the worker for assistance. "What would you do?" the guest speaker asked the class. All but one of the exceedingly helpful students stated that they would try to help move the tree trunk off the man. "But what happens when you get trapped by the tree, as well?" asked the speaker. "We'd get help," answered the students. "But by then," the speaker enjoined, "it would be too late." The lesson, of course, is that caseworkers and social workers often go into the field precisely because of their wish to help others. What they learn throughout the course of their educational training, hopefully, is that sometimes the most helpful thing you can do is to not be too helpful. Clients need to be encouraged to do the necessary work to accomplish their goals. Workers, in their wish to be helpful, cannot only lose opportunities to help clients to discover their own resourcefulness, but also exhaust themselves in the process. As a caseworker, it is important to ask others for help and not to think that you must do everything yourself. It is important to leave the problems of the workplace at the office door, and incorporate activities that are fun and stress-relieving into your personal routine.

Over-Involvement of Worker

At other times, workers may be over-involved with their clients. Over-involvement may be expressed through such behaviors as an overidentification with the client's feelings and problems, lack of emotional distance, distortion in perceiving the extent of the client's difficulty, colluding with the client's efforts to sabotage resolution of problems, or an avoidance of challenging or confronting a client whose behavior is clearly counter to the attainment of goals. Another all too common manifestation of a worker's over-involvement with a client concerns boundary violations. This occurs when the worker is unable to maintain a professional role with a client and becomes personally involved as a friend or sexual partner. Younger workers may be particularly vulnerable to boundary violations when they are working with clients who are close to their age. If you find yourself becoming attracted to your client and experience difficulty maintaining professional boundaries, you should immediately seek supervision. If you think that you are at risk for a boundary violation, you should consider transferring the client to another worker.

Cross-Racial and Cross-Cultural Barriers

Barriers to change can occur when the worker and client are identified with different racial groups. For example, an African American woman may find it difficult to work with a Caucasian woman, as she may feel that the worker cannot understand her experience of living in a society that privileges Whites.

Barriers can also occur when workers impose their own cultural values and beliefs on their clients, rather than understanding that clients may have a different cultural perspective and viewpoint from their workers. For example, when working with clients from Caribbean countries, it is important to keep in mind that adult children may feel a cultural obligation to care for parents, even if the parent appears to be abusive or destructive to a client's well-being and livelihood. Indeed, in cultures that value embedded family connections and relationships, westernized notions of separation and autonomy may be anathema to the cultural values and beliefs of the client.

Working with Sexual Minorities

The NASW code of ethics explicitly bans discrimination on the basis of sexual orientation and encourages social workers to act to expand access, choices, and opportunities for oppressed people and groups. Sexual minorities include those individuals who identify as lesbian, gay, bisexual, transgendered, queer, or intersexed. According to NASW, "Social workers need to understand the complex issues that lesbian, gay, and bisexual people encounter within the dominant culture in order to provide services respectful of each individual" (2003b, 224). Nonetheless, many human service workers experience bias toward sexual minorities.

Fassinger (1991) found that many psychotherapists, including social workers, are ill informed about the issues facing sexual minorities and hold heterosexist assumptions and cultural stereotypes about sexual minorities. These assumptions and stereotypes are believed to be rooted in institutional arrangements where sexual minorities are subjected to discrimination in housing, employment, access to adequate mental health and healthcare, social services, and immigration and naturalization services. Societal discrimination against sexual minorities is believed to be based on homophobism, defined as "the irrational hatred, fear, and stereotyping of those whose primary sexual and affectional orientation is toward people of their own gender" (NASW 2003b, 227). Human service professionals need to be vigilant about examining their underlying attitudes, feelings, and assumptions about working with sexual minorities and work toward increasing their understanding of sexual minority cultures.

Difficulty in Establishing Trust

When clients who have great difficulty trusting others come in for professional support and services, it is often very difficult for them to express vulnerability or relinquish any sense of control over their welfare to another. These patients may require help in understanding this conflict before they are willing or able to enter into a trusting relationship with their worker.

For some clients, trusting the worker—or depending upon anyone, for that matter—is extremely fraught with difficulty. For example, some clients come to an agency for assistance precisely because they have become emotionally and/or financially depleted through their seemingly boundless efforts to care for others. These clients are often considered to be the "rocks" in their families and social networks, the people that others consistently rely upon, trust with confidences, and look to for advice on the problems of life. Often, these clients have vicariously met their own emotional needs by tending to the needs of others.

Mandated clients may also have great difficulty trusting their workers. They may have been told that they will lose visitation privileges or custody of their children if they don't attend parenting counseling, for example, and may perceive the worker as an agent for the court or as having a vested interest in someone other than the client. Similarly, clients who are mandated to come in for counseling by their employers due to job-related difficulties may experience challenges in trusting that the worker is not representing the interests of the employer.

It is important for workers to recognize that their first commitment is to the client and to protecting the client's best interests, but sometimes that commitment is mediated by a need to protect the rights of others, including children and the community at large. For example, if you are working with a mandated client who wishes to regain custody of her children but is not coming to her mandated sessions or following through with other required tasks, such as attending parenting classes, you may be forced to disclose this information to the Court's representative, because the potential safety of the children is at stake. In this case, the rights of the minor child to protection supersede the rights of the client to confidentiality. However, in order to maintain your professional commitment to the mother, you would likely inform her at the beginning of your work together that you are obligated to report whether or not she is attending sessions. Your primary professional commitment remains with the client, not the court. Your responsibility is to support the client as best as you can in her goal to regain custody.

Transference and Countertransference

Workers need to be cognizant of transference and countertransference issues that may arise in their work with clients. If the worker is not aware of them, they can pose a barrier to the working relationship or alliance. There are times when workers may wish to explore transference issues with the client. At other times, a worker may need to respond to a client who declares that the worker does not perceive the client accurately.

Transference

Transference occurs when the client attributes to the worker aspects of important figures from the client's past. Clients may attribute to the worker the same traits, feelings, and beliefs possessed by significant others from their past. Feelings associated with this significant figure may thus be experienced in the present transference relationship. If these relationships were fraught with conflict or were otherwise deemed by the client to be unhealthy or dysfunctional, the worker may be hampered in his or her ability to foster a good working relationship with the client.

Despite the barriers posed by the client's transference reactions toward the worker, they may also offer opportunities to explore the problematic nature of the client's interpersonal relationships and thus support the development of a good working relationship. Moreover, a positive transference can help to lay the groundwork for a good working relationship. Workers should be aware, however, that sometimes clients will view them as omnipotent helpers and rescuers. If this occurs (and despite the obvious ego boost that this can provide) the worker should be careful to avoid the pitfall of attempting to become the "all good" transference figure. Otherwise, the worker will not be supporting the client's self-determination and may be setting him- or herself up for compassion fatigue.

Examples of Transference Phenomena

▶ A client who was brought up by a rejecting parent experiences everything you say and do as further evidence of your lack of concern for him.

▶ A client who had a positive relationship with her mother immediately establishes a positive rapport with her female caseworker.

Countertransference

Conversely, countertransference occurs when workers experience their clients as possessing the traits and motivations of important figures from their past. This can sometimes hinder the worker from seeing the client clearly and can impede the development of an effective working relationship. At other times, countertransference may also be a real reaction to the client and a source of valuable information about the client.

To the extent that the worker is aware of his or her countertransferential sensitivities, the worker should be able to distinguish between real aspects of the client and significant persons from the worker's past. If the worker finds that he or she cannot overcome countertransferential reactions to the client through supervision or self-analysis, then the worker may wish to consider transferring the client to another helper. The worker may also consider seeking his or her own counseling or therapy in order to address unresolved countertransference issues.

Examples of Countertransference Phenomena

▶ A worker who had a very authoritarian father finds it difficult to challenge her older male client.

▶ A worker who was recently divorced finds herself immediately siding with her female patient, who is undergoing marital difficulties.

Cultural Transference and Countertransference

Cultural transference and countertransference phenomena are also very important areas to consider when working with individuals from diverse backgrounds. Cultural transference and countertransference can become issues even when working with individuals who are from the same cultural, ethnic, or racial background as your own.

Comas-Díaz and Jacobsen (1991) have identified four types of transference and countertransference phenomena that may occur between workers and clients. These include interethnic transference and countertransference, and intra-ethnic transference and countertransference.

Interethnic transference and countertransference occur when you are working with individuals from a different cultural background from you; intra-ethnic transference and countertransference occurs when you are working with individuals from similar cultural backgrounds to yours. The following are some examples of interethnic transference and countertransference.

Interethnic Transference

Overcompliance and friendliness: This may be represented by a client deferring to the wishes of the worker, despite his or her misgivings about a particular course of action, or when a client idealizes a worker on the basis of the worker's cultural background. This can also occur if a client is overcompensating for his or her distrust of a worker based upon cultural differences. In any case, this type of transference interferes with the development of a true working alliance, in that the client is unable to bring in his or her true feelings and thoughts to the working relationship.

Denial of ethnicity and culture: This may occur when a client denies any cultural differences between him- or herself and the worker. This might occur if the client is uncomfortable with the idea that there is a cultural or ethnic difference, and may be a way to avoid a discussion of potential bias. Moreover, in a culture that has promoted the notion of "color blindness," clients may fear that it is impolite or even discriminatory to possess awareness of cultural or ethnic difference.

Mistrust, suspicion, and hostility: Sometimes clients' own cultural stereotypes or prejudices may be revealed through their mistrust, suspicion, or hostility of the worker. For example, the client may have experienced discrimination from others from a similar cultural, ethnic, or racial background as the worker, or may perceive that the worker holds prejudicial ideas about the client.

Ambivalence: The client may hold conflicted feelings toward the worker. For example, he or she may wish to trust the worker, but may also have feelings of apprehension as to whether this trust is warranted. Also, clients sometimes experience pressures from members of their own ethnic groups, who may advise them to work only with workers who are from the same ethnic or racial group as their own.

Interethnic Countertransference

Denial of ethno-cultural differences: This type of countertransference occurs when the worker chooses not to notice or address the ethnic or cultural differences that exist in the worker-client dyad. This can prevent the worker from exploring issues that may impede the creation of a working relationship.

Cultural detective syndrome: When the worker uses the opportunity of working with a client from a different ethno-cultural background to find out information about a particular population or group, this may be considered an example of the cultural detective syndrome. Typically, when this type of countertransference occurs, the worker is seeking to satisfy his or her curiosity, rather than focus attention on what the client may be feeling or on issues that the client may be bringing into the interview.

Guilt: If a worker feels guilt toward a particular ethnic, cultural, or racial group because of the prejudices the group has faced at the hands of the dominant group, with whom the worker may identify, he or she may have difficulty confronting the client about destructive behaviors or attitudes, or may collude or join with a client's defense mechanisms of denial or avoidance.

Pity: Workers may find themselves feeling sorry for the experiences they imagine that a client has undergone due to his or her particular ethno-cultural background. These perceptions on the part of the worker may not accurately reflect the actual experiences that the client has had.

Aggression: Workers who are unaware of their use of cultural stereotypes or bias toward particular ethno-cultural groups may express hostility and anger toward a client who is a representative of that particular ethno-cultural group.

Ambivalence: A worker may experience conflicts about working with a client from a particular background. They may wish to be of help and yet, at the same time, feel a reluctance to work with a particular client.

Intra-Ethnic Transference
Omniscient-omnipotent therapist: Sometimes clients may view workers who hail from a similar cultural background as their own as being all-knowing and powerful.

The traitor: Clients may sometimes believe that workers who have achieved higher education or success have "sold out" to mainstream interests and forgotten their cultural, ethnic, or racial roots.

The auto-racist: This kind of transference may occur if the client feels that the worker views him- or herself as inferior on the basis of his or her cultural or ethnic identity. The client may then fear that the worker will look down on him or her because of the similarity of their backgrounds.

Ambivalence: A client may feel conflicted about a worker who is from the same cultural background as their own and may have mixed feelings about working with him or her.

Intra-Ethnic Countertransference
Overidentification: Workers may inaccurately perceive that clients who are members of their particular ethno-cultural group may have had similar experiences to their own, or hold similar beliefs or attitudes about life.

Us and them (collusion): When workers overidentify with the struggles of their clients, they may enter into relationships with them where all responsibility for difficulties is projected onto the environment.

Distancing: Workers may find themselves emotionally distancing themselves in their work with clients from similar backgrounds. This may seem counterintuitive, but workers may have unresolved issues about their own ethno-cultural experiences and thus be reluctant to explore these issues with their clients.

Cultural myopia: Workers may lose their perspective about the kinds of issues that their clients are facing because they haven't yet worked out their own ethno-cultural issues.

Anger: Unresolved ethno-cultural issues of workers may be reflected in ongoing anger toward individuals from their own background who they may feel have perpetuated cultural stereotypes against them. This anger can sometimes be directed toward a client from a similar background.

Survivor guilt: A worker may feel a sense of guilt that he or she has been able to transcend the oppressive forces of discrimination, and attain a level of professional respectability that the client has not had an opportunity to achieve.

Hope and despair: A worker may both feel hope that the client's situation will improve and the client will learn to thrive despite societal biases, and also experience despair that the client will be ever be successful in overcoming discriminatory cultural practices. To the extent that workers are aware of countertransferential pitfalls, they may be better able to avoid them or identify them when they arise.

Splitting and Projective Identification

Splitting and projective identification are terms identified in the literature as psychological defense mechanisms used primarily by individuals who have not yet fully achieved integrated perceptions of self and others. These terms originally emanated from the field of object relations theory. The use of splitting and projective identification by clients can present great challenges to the workers who are treating them. These defenses also occur in the personal lives of these clients and often contribute to their presenting issues.

Splitting occurs when the client views individuals, both self and others, as either all good or all bad. There is nothing in between. The client has not yet developed to the point where he or she recognizes that all people have both positive and negative traits. Thus, workers may be perceived as entirely good or entirely bad. This can be difficult for the caseworker, particularly if he or she has become perceived by the client as all bad, because he or she can do nothing right in the eyes of the client.

Individuals who use splitting as a psychological defense also tend to put staff members into all good or all bad camps. On an agency level, this can cause problems when staff members differ in their perceptions of clients, as the client shows very different sides of him- or herself to staff members depending upon whether they are perceived as all good or all bad. If workers and staff members understand processes of splitting, and the proclivity of some clients to engage in it, it then becomes possible for staff to resist these processes, as well as help the client begin to achieve a more integrated view of self and others.

Projective identification often occurs in tandem with splitting and may be defined as a process by which the client projects or attributes unwanted aspects of him- or herself or others into the worker, and the worker actually comes to feel as if he or she has become transformed into another person. Thus, for example, a worker may come to feel exceedingly angry toward a client who has a history of being mistreated by parents and others. The client may be unwittingly behaving in a way that causes the worker to become increasingly frustrated and annoyed. For example, a client may repeatedly call a worker between sessions, or forget to bring the payment, or consistently berate the worker, ridiculing the worker on his or her choice of dress or office décor. The challenge for the worker is to resist acting out his or her anger (i.e., becoming the "mistreating parent") and instead help the client to understand how and why the client is provoking the worker.

RECORD-KEEPING PROCEDURES

In addition to learning skills of interviewing, and establishing and maintaining effective client relationships, caseworkers must also keep accurate and detailed records of clients and their professional contacts with them. Increasingly, and to the chagrin of many caseworkers, the completion of timely paperwork continues to be a principal component of the caseworker's duties. The primary reason for keeping accurate client records and documenting all client contacts is to ensure compliance with legal and administrative dictates. For example, in terms of legal mandates, you must be able to demonstrate that you performed the service for which the client is being billed. Administratively, you must also be able to document all services provided to the client on behalf of the agency. To some extent, the increased emphasis on record-keeping and accountability flies in the face of what many consider to be the mainstay of the human service professional, which is to provide quality services to clients on a case-by-case basis. Too much time spent on ensuring accountability or on documenting the effectiveness of services can deplete the time available to actually provide effective services.

Components of Case Notes

Contact notes should always include the focus of the interview; a concise assessment of the client's behavior, appearance and emotional presentation, or affect; the resolution of the interview, if appropriate; and the reason for and date of the next client contact and with whom the client will be meeting. Summers (2006) offers the following guidelines for keeping records of client contacts within agency work:

> **Identifying the Specific Contact.** Many forms used by agencies include a space in the left-hand column to specify the date and the type of contact. Examples of types of contact include collateral contact, office visit, phone contact, site visit, or home visit.

Collateral contact refers to a visit with someone other than the client, such as the client's parent or spouse. In most cases, any contact with a collateral person requires permission from the client. Exceptions include the worker's "duty to warn," when dealing with a suicidal or homicidal client. This will be explained more fully when discussing ethical considerations.

Documenting Collateral Service Provision. If you are working in the capacity of a case manager, you must document your efforts to ensure that collateral agencies are following through with their portion of services specified in the treatment plan. All phone calls with other service providers or in-person meetings should be documented in the records and labeled accordingly in the left-hand margin of the case note (e.g., phone call or site visit) (Summers 2006, 332–333).

The Use of Professional Language in Record Keeping

Summers (2006, 334–336) suggests the following tips for writing professional notes:

- ▶ Avoid hostility.
- ▶ Document all interactions with clients.
- ▶ Document important aspects of the contact.
- ▶ Be clear and precise.
- ▶ Use language clients can understand.

Government Rules

State and local governments require that certain rules be followed when writing up case notes and records (Summers 2006). Some of these rules include the following:

- ▶ Always use black ink.
- ▶ Do not use correction fluid or pencil when writing notes.

- ▶ Write legibly.
- ▶ The client's name or identification number must be included on each page of the record.
- ▶ Always date each note that is placed in the record.
- ▶ Sign your full name and indicate date of signature on each case note.
- ▶ If the client is in ongoing contact with the agency, be sure to include the date of the next visit at the end of the note.
- ▶ If it is necessary to correct a note, cross out the error with a single line, initial it, write the word "error" next to the line, make the appropriate change, and initial and date the correction.
- ▶ Draw lines through any blank pages in the record (Summers 2006, 337–338).

Maintaining Confidentiality of Client Records

It is imperative that caseworkers follow careful record-keeping procedures that protect the confidentiality of clients. Funding sources, accrediting bodies, and state and federal laws may all specify the manner in which client records may be maintained. Additionally, the trend of maintaining computerized client records may make the records more susceptible to unauthorized access. Furthermore, keep in mind that client records may be subpoenaed and that you and your agency will need to justify your and the agencies actions.

The following guidelines, adapted from Hepworth et al. (2006, 71–72) may be used to maintain confidentiality of client records:

Ethics of Professional Practice

The ethics of social work practice have come a long way since the days when early caseworkers were interested in remediating the moral deficiencies of individuals and families. Now human service professionals are much more likely to focus on the morals inherent in their own profession and to identify ways to recognize and resolve complex moral and ethical dilemmas. Today, almost all human service professionals are required to abide by certain ethical standards. Ethical standards typically flow from the underlying values that are considered important to any given culture. The ethical principles and standards of professional practice have been developed to ensure that service recipients will be treated in a safe and trustworthy manner.

This is especially important because many individuals who seek or are mandated to receive services are vulnerable and in a position where they can be exploited by others, especially those whom they come to depend upon, such as their caseworkers. They are likely to be sharing personal and deeply intimate details of their lives. Indeed, clients often reveal aspects of their lives to their caseworkers that they wouldn't normally share with anyone else. Thus, human service workers must behave in an absolutely trustworthy and ethical manner.

Holland and Kilpatrick (1991, 138) put it well when they said:

> Social work exists because society is concerned about the vulnerable, the disenfranchised, the isolated, and the suffering. Most social services are carried out through organizations that structure and focus the actions of staff and that represent society's concern for the needy. The commodity entrusts power to social workers and others in such programs to use its resources and to implement delivery of services with caring and integrity.

Most professional organizations that govern the helping professions have developed a code of ethics that must be followed by their member constituents. For example, both the National Organization for Human Services (NOHS) and the National Association of Social Workers have issued written ethical codes that may be used as guidelines in resolving ethical conflicts and dilemmas and may serve as a standard of practice in a legal matter. Indeed, the NASW (1999) code of ethics now specifies 155 ethical standards to guide professional social work practice. These standards provide guidelines that may be used in identifying and resolving ethical dilemmas, applying value-based problem-solving strategies, managing ethical issues that could lead to litigation, and regulating ethical misconduct within the profession. Moreover, these ethical codes are often considered as benchmarks of appropriate professional conduct by state licensing and regulatory boards, providers of professional liability insurance, the courts, and private and governmental agencies (Reamer 1998). Some of these guidelines have previously been discussed in earlier sections of this chapter. Several other guidelines will now be discussed in greater depth.

Dual Relationships

The NASW code of ethics specifies the following with regard to dual or multiple relationships:

> Social workers should not engage in dual or multiple relation-
> ships with clients or former clients in which there is a risk of ex-
> ploitation or potential harm to the client. In instances when dual
> or multiple relationships are unavoidable, social workers should
> take steps to protect clients and are responsible for setting clear,
> appropriate, and culturally sensitive boundaries (Dual or multiple
> relationships occur when social workers relate to clients in more
> than one relationship, whether professional, social, or business.
> Dual or multiple relationships can occur simultaneously or con-
> secutively.) (NASW 1999).

Human service workers should avoid potential conflicts of interest when working with clients, which may occur if they become involved in dual relationships. A dual relationship presents the possibility of exploitation of a client, or vice versa, and should be avoided whenever possible. For example, a dual relationship of a personal nature would exist if you accepted an invitation to attend a ball game or some other social event with a client. Such a relationship might compromise your professional judgment or cause you to have ethical dilemmas if the client, for example, seeks special privileges or favors from you.

Conversely, if you asked a client for tickets to a sold-out ball game that your children may wish to attend, the client may worry that, if he or she doesn't comply with your request, there may be repercussions that affect him or her in the securing of needed resources you are overseeing.

A dual professional relationship would exist if you served as both your client's income eligibility caseworker, for example, and also as his or her protective services caseworker. You may, for example, discover that your ability to be impartial and objective is tainted by your prior professional relationship with that client. Similarly, if you hired a client to clean your home or perform any professional or business service for you, this would be considered a dual relationship and would be ethically unacceptable. Again, the client may feel that he or she can't say no to your request, or you may be hampered in your ability to apply fair and impartial standards in your professional dealings with the client or the client's family.

If you live in a small town or community, these guidelines may not always be possible to uphold. For example, you may find that you are serving on the same parent-teacher association as one of your clients, or your client may also be working for the tax collection department of your village. In cases where you cannot avoid a dual relationship with a client, it is important to explore whether or not, under the circumstance, the client wishes to continue to work with you, or if a referral to another caseworker may be warranted.

Sexual Relationships

NASW specifies the following in regard to sexual relationships with clients, former clients, or providing services to someone with whom you have had a sexual relationship:

> ▶ "Social workers should under no circumstances engage in sexual activities or sexual contact with current clients, whether such contact is consensual or forced.
> ▶ Social workers should not engage in sexual activities or sexual contact with clients' relatives or other individuals with whom clients maintain a close personal relationship when there is a risk of exploitation or potential harm to the client. Sexual activity or sexual contact with clients' relatives or other individuals with whom clients maintain a personal relationship has the potential to be harmful to the client and may make it difficult for the social worker and client to maintain appropriate professional boundaries. Social workers—not their clients, their clients' relatives, or other individuals with whom the client maintains a personal relationship—assume the full burden for setting clear, appropriate, and culturally sensitive boundaries.
> ▶ Social workers should not engage in sexual activities or sexual contact with former clients because of the potential for harm to the

client. If social workers engage in conduct contrary to this prohibition or claim that an exception to this prohibition is warranted because of extraordinary circumstances, it is social workers—not their clients—who assume the full burden of demonstrating that the former client has not been exploited, coerced, or manipulated, intentionally or unintentionally.

► Social workers should not provide clinical services to individuals with whom they have had a prior sexual relationship. Providing clinical services to a former sexual partner has the potential to be harmful to the individual and is likely to make it difficult for the social worker and individual to maintain appropriate professional boundaries" (NASW 1999).

Despite the way the media and entertainment industry has, at times, portrayed therapists and social workers becoming romantically or sexually involved with clients, clients' spouses, or clients' relatives, human service workers are strictly prohibited from engaging in sexual relationships with their clients. Both the National Organization for Human Services and the National Association of Social Workers provide ethical guidelines that explicitly prohibit any sexual relationships between workers and current or former clients.

Caseworkers need to be sensitive to any warning signs that suggest they may be having difficulty maintaining professional boundaries with particular clients. These warning signs might include such things as thinking excessively about a client during off-work hours, dressing in a provocative or special way in anticipation of seeing a specific client, having frequent dreams about a client (this may indicate countertransference feelings), or making extra or unnecessary appointments with a client. If you have reason to suspect that a colleague may be involved personally with a client, or at risk of committing a boundary violation, you have a professional responsibility to speak to him or her and encourage that supervision is sought. You may also need to consider reporting this colleague to your supervisor, the professional licensing board, or the professional member organization that oversees your particular profession (e.g., NASW or NOHS).

If any of these or other warning signs exist, you should immediately consult with your supervisor. Workers may be more vulnerable to losing sight of professional boundaries when they are undergoing stressful times in their lives or are experiencing burnout. Not only is becoming sexually involved with a client destructive to your client, it can also be destructive to you. You could lose your job and even destroy your professional career. If you experience difficulty maintaining professional boundaries with a client, despite supervisory consultation, you may need to think about transferring the case to another worker.

On the other hand, clients may, at times, mistakenly think that you are a potential romantic partner for them. They may misinterpret your attention and empathy toward them as evidence of your affection or romantic interest, and may believe that you will marry them or otherwise become personally involved with them. It is important to be aware of this when working with clients, and quickly dispel any misunderstandings that may develop. Clients are very vulnerable and may quickly form erotic transferences toward their workers. Caseworkers must be clear in maintaining professional boundaries both in order to protect their clients and also themselves from disastrous, even tragic consequences. Worker burnout can also place workers at greater risk of committing boundary violations with clients. Regular supervision can be enormously helpful in supporting the work and preventing the occurrence of boundary violations.

Self-Determination

NASW offers the following statement regarding self-determination in the code of ethics:

> Social workers respect and promote the right of clients to self-determination and assist clients in their efforts to identify and clarify their goals. Social workers may limit clients' right to self-determination when, in the social workers' professional judgment, clients' actions or potential actions pose a serious, foreseeable, and imminent risk to themselves or others (NASW 1999).

Self-determination is an important value in casework and social work practice. With the advent of strengths-based practice, which has virtually changed the paradigm within which much casework is now delivered, self-determination has moved even more into the forefront. Clients have the right to be informed about the kinds of services they will be receiving and, in many cases, are now required by government and other regulatory bodies to sign off on treatment and other service plans.

Moreover, clients have the right to establish their own objectives and goals, although this is usually done in consultation with their workers, and, except in the case of mandated services, to decide how long they will stay with an agency, and when and whether they no longer wish to receive services. Clients in mental health settings have the right to be informed about the diagnosis they will be given and to participate in decisions concerning the kind of treatment they will receive for their diagnoses.

However, as indicated in the NASW code of ethics, the client's right to self-determination may be limited in cases where the safety and protection of either the client or society would be compromised by this right. Superseding a client's right to self-determination may be acceptable, for example, in cases where the client is under the legal age of consent, when a client is deemed incompetent, or when a client is a danger to him- or herself and/or others. Furthermore, Mattaini (2002) makes the interesting point that in some cultures, the good of the group trumps the good of the individual, so that a client's right to self-determination may also need to be interpreted within a cultural frame of reference.

Confidentiality

Confidentiality is absolutely required for good casework practice, and NASW (1999) has issued a protracted statement on the ways in which confidentiality must be ensured by helping professionals. A general principle is that client information should be shared only with those with a "need to know." For example, client names or any other identifying information about a client should not be shared in group supervision. At times, however, there are limits to confidentiality.

Limits to Confidentiality

There are exceptions to the client's right to confidentiality. Under certain circumstances, workers may be compelled to reveal information about the client with whom they are working. These circumstances include supervision and consultation, when clients have waived their right to confidentiality, when the client poses a danger to self or others, if there is a suspicion of elder or child abuse and neglect, or when the courts subpoena client records.

With regard to the client posing a danger to self or others, the caseworker has a legal obligation to inform the individual or individuals who may be at risk of bodily harm, individuals who may be in a position to warn the intended victim, and the police. This duty to warn was established through a 1976 case brought before the California Supreme Court, *Tarasoff v. Regents of University of California*, which concluded that ". . . the confidential character of the patient-psychotherapist communication must yield to the extent to which disclosure is essential to avert danger to others. The protective privilege ends where the public peril begins." This duty to protect extends to human service workers as well as therapists.

Other instances in which the client's right to confidentiality may be suspended include when the client needs emergency medical services, such as in the case of an overdose, or if you are attempting to collect payment for services rendered, after having exhausted all other avenues of collecting payment.

HIPAA Rules and Regulations

The Health Insurance Portability and Accountability Act (HIPAA), passed into law in 1996, was created to help ensure that individuals would be able to maintain their medical insurance when they changed jobs. However, Title II of the act contains stringent rules and procedures for maintaining privacy of individuals' medical records. Most individuals were not affected by HIPAA regulations until 2003, when all insurance carriers, agencies, and service providers were mandated to comply with the law. Most agencies that provide social services to clients provide training to employees on HIPAA regulations. Individuals and organizations that do not adhere to HIPAA regulations face stiff fines and even prison time. HIPAA rules apply to formal records, as well as personal case notes and billing information. Many practitioners believe that the rules don't go far enough in protecting client records, particularly in terms of providing sensitive information to insurance companies and government employees. The United States Department of

Health and Human Services provides the following information about HIPAA:

"A major goal of the Privacy Rule is to assure that individuals' health information is properly protected while allowing the flow of health information needed to provide and promote high quality healthcare and to protect the public's health and well being. The Rule strikes a balance that permits important uses of information, while protecting the privacy of people who seek care and healing. Given that the healthcare marketplace is diverse; the Rule is designed to be flexible and comprehensive to cover the variety of uses and disclosures that need to be addressed" (U.S. Department of Health and Human Services 2003).

Some of the main provisions of the bill include the following:

- Agencies must comply with privacy rules.
- Agencies must develop a system to maintain confidentiality of records.
- Agencies must provide training to staff on HIPAA regulations.
- Agencies must provide all clients with copies of the privacy rules of the agency and under which circumstances information in client files may be released.
- Clients have the right to read their records, make copies of their files, and make corrections to their files.
- Clients must be given a form to sign that indicates that they received information on the agency's confidentiality.

In addition to these guidelines, extra care must be taken to ensure the privacy and security of clients and their records. Thus, accessibility to client files must be limited to only those who have jurisdiction over the case. Work areas and storage areas must be secured. Discussion of clients should only take place in areas where others can't overhear what is being said. Receptionists must be discreet when using clients' names and other identifying information in public waiting rooms. Security measures must be instituted to protect electronic files.

CHAPTER three

SPECIAL AREAS OF SOCIAL WORK KNOWLEDGE

ENTRY-LEVEL SOCIAL workers with associate's or bachelor's degrees are usually prepared academically to perform as generalists and are able to provide services to a broad range of clients, within a variety of practice settings. They often possess a wide knowledge base, and are able to practice using a diversity of skills. Advanced practitioners with graduate-level education may be prepared to practice as advanced generalist practitioners who are trained to work across a range of system levels, including work with individuals, groups, organizations, and communities. Advanced practitioners may also specialize in areas such as clinical, medical, or school social work, planning and development, aging, mental health, or corrections.

Thus, one of the advantages of a career in casework is that one may choose to work in a number of specialized areas. Although particular skill sets may be germane to specific fields of practice, many of these skills are general enough that they may be transferred across areas of specialization. Indeed, social workers may change their particular areas of specialization several times throughout their careers, thus keeping their work varied, interesting, and challenging. This chapter will introduce you to several of these specialized areas of practice, including public healthcare, social work with children, and public housing and assistance programs. You will also become acquainted with a beginning overview of the knowledge base necessary to effectively carry out casework within these diverse settings.

PUBLIC HEALTH

Before beginning a discussion of the specialized area of social work in public health, it is important to note a distinction between "healthcare" and "medical care." According to Cowles (2000, 13), "Medical care is what physicians provide in the course of monitoring patient health and diagnosing and treating health problems; Healthcare refers to individual and societal efforts to prevent health problems from emerging and to maintain current levels of health."

Thus, healthcare necessitates both assuming personal responsibility for one's health through proper diet and exercise, adequate sleep, taking safety precautions, etc., and also through society's responsibility to provide a safe, supportive, and pollution-free environment (Cowles 2000). Along these same lines, The World Health Organization (WHO) has developed a holistic definition of health as "a state of complete physical, mental, and social well-being and not merely the absence of disease or infirmity" (World Health Organization 1958). Dhooper (1997, 74) further explains:

> "The terms public and health provide the themes for what public health is all about. Public does not refer to the auspices under which a program is carried out, but rather to the public it serves. The agency providing services may be governmental or voluntary and private. Public also involves organized community effort. Individual effort is important but must be augmented by community-wide work. . . ."

To illustrate this point, Dhooper provides the example of smoking. He points to the improved health benefits achieved by the reduction of smoking in public places made possible by community efforts to institute laws and regulations restricting smoking. At its core, public health encompasses notions of social justice and the protection of life for the entire community. In summary, the mission of public health is the promotion and maintenance of health for the entire populace.

What is public health? How is it different from healthcare? According to the Council of State Governments (n.d., paragraph 2):

"In public health, the goal is to prevent disease or injury in a whole population—a city, state, or country, for example. That's different from the goal of healthcare, which is to care for individuals. An example may make the distinction sharper: a public health approach to cancer could involve a statewide public awareness campaign about the risk factors for cancer such as smoking or sun exposure, while a healthcare approach would focus on educating individuals about such risk factors."

The American Public Health Association (APHA) defines public health as follows:

▶ Public health is the practice of preventing disease and promoting good health within groups of people, from small communities to entire countries.
▶ Public Health is Policy Development and Population Health Surveillance.
▶ Public health professionals rely on policy and research strategies to understand issues such as infant mortality and chronic disease in particular populations.

Why It's Important

Public Health Saves Money and Improves Quality of Life. A healthy public gets sick less frequently and spends less money on healthcare; this means better economic productivity and an improved quality of life for everyone.

Improving Public Health Helps Children Thrive. Healthy children become healthy adults. Healthy kids attend school more often and perform better overall. Public health professionals strive to ensure that all kids grow up in a healthy environment with adequate resources, including healthcare.

Public Health Prevention Reduces Human Suffering. Public health prevention not only educates people about the effects of lifestyle choices on their health, but also reduces the impact of disasters by preparing people for the effects of catastrophes such as hurricanes, tornadoes, and terrorist attacks.

Public Health as a Profession. Rather than being a single discipline, public health includes professionals from many fields with the common purpose of protecting the health of a population. These professionals include emergency responders, restaurant inspectors, health educators, public policymakers, scientists and researchers, public health physicians, public health nurses, occupational health and safety professionals, social workers, sanitarians, epidemiologists, nutritionists, community planners. (American Public Health Association n.d., a)

Social Work and Public Health

The profession of social work has been involved with public healthcare since its earliest inception. Indeed, social work's earliest specialization was in the area of healthcare. The evolution of healthcare in the United States has gone through several phases in its development; the earliest incarnation being the almshouses of the 1700s.

The first almshouses were built to offer refuge to the poor, the sick, and the mentally ill. Often dirty and extremely poorly run, these almshouses or "poorhouses" became known as places of death for society's misbegotten. The healthcare workers who provided help to these outcasts of society, many of whom were destitute and suffered from contagious diseases, often became ill themselves due to the unsanitary conditions of these facilities. The almshouse, a community-based institution, is often viewed as "the fore-runner to today's hospitals" (Dziegielewski 2004, 49). However, it wasn't until the theory of germs was developed at the turn of the twentieth century that the focus of individual illness and disability turned toward environmental and medical causes. Up until that time, dirt, sloth, and uncleanliness were deemed the primary causes of illness and infirmity, and individuals were held responsible for their own health problems.

According to the National Association of Social Workers (2005), early social workers were concerned with supporting the availability of healthcare services for the poor and the amelioration of social conditions that bred infectious diseases. Later, social workers joined forces with other healthcare professionals in the drive to provide quality systems of public healthcare. Today, caseworkers and social workers are involved in almost every area of public healthcare provision. The National Association of Social Workers has issued the following policy statement on social work and public health:

> "the purposes of social work in healthcare is threefold: to assist individuals, their families, and significant others to function when illness, disease, or disability results in changes in their physical state, mental state or social roles; to prevent social and emotional problems from interfering with physical and mental or with needed treatment; and to identify gaps in community services and to work with community-based agencies and institutions to expand the capacity of the community to provide adequate supports" (2003, 168–169).

The changing landscapes of healthcare financing and service delivery systems are presenting new challenges and opportunities to caseworkers and social workers who choose to work in the field of public health with limited public funding and stigmatized clients who are the "new undeserving" (e.g., uninsured). Some professionals are calling for advanced specialty training for hospital work, while others are calling for more specializations within the field of healthcare (e.g., gerontology and infant health), as well as an expanded use of knowledge-based practices to ensure quality services in these tumultuous and changing times (Keigher 1997).

Current Status of Healthcare

In 2005, the National Association of Social Workers issued a comprehensive statement on the current state of healthcare in America and specified standards of practice that social workers in healthcare settings should follow:

The constant growth, demands, and changes in healthcare have had a serious impact on the viability and need for social workers in all areas and settings of healthcare. As of 2006, there were 47 million Americans, or 15.8% of the population, without any health insurance coverage (U.S. Census Bureau, 2007). Access to timely, comprehensive, and equitable healthcare for individuals in the United States varies considerably, with significant percentages of many populations having only limited access to healthcare.

The growth in medical technology has offered hope and improved quality of life to many people; yet, the advances in technology have also raised healthcare costs and introduced social, legal, and ethical dilemmas for individuals, families, and healthcare providers. These psychosocial implications of healthcare are what social workers are trained to address.

Currently, healthcare social workers provide services across the continuum of care and in various settings. Social workers are present in public health, acute and chronic care settings providing a range of services including health education, crisis intervention, supportive counseling, and case management. In response to critical incidents that are both global and national, healthcare social workers are increasingly trained to provide interventions to prepare for and respond to traumatic events and disasters.

The healthcare system in the United States is complex and multidisciplinary in nature, and may include a network of services such as diagnosis, treatment, rehabilitation, health maintenance and prevention provided to individuals of all ages and with a range of needs. Multiple sources of financing, ranging from Medicare and Medicaid to private insurance, provide further challenges. Many consumers lack health insurance or have inadequate coverage, which causes financial stress on consumers and providers. Professional social workers are well equipped to practice in the healthcare field because of their broad perspective on the range of physical, emotional, and environmental factors that have an effect on the well-being of individuals and communities (NASW 2005, 5–6).

The Rise of Managed Care: An Overview[1]

In the last 20 years, the ascendance of managed care organizations (MCOs) has revolutionized the ways that health and mental healthcare are financed, structured, and provided. Increasingly, clinical social workers have replaced medical and other nonmedical practitioners as the more cost-effective and, therefore, preferred providers of mental health services in managed care settings (Cohen 2003).

Shapiro (1995, 441) has defined managed care as "any kind of healthcare services which are paid for, all, or in part, by a third party (including any government entity) and for which the focus of any part of clinical decision-making is other than between the practitioner and the client or patient." Managed care systems are increasingly used to treat clients insured by public social services, many of which are being privatized (Packard 1989). Mechanic, Schlesinger, and McAlpine (1995, 2) explained that the main objective of managed care is to "limit unnecessary medical utilization while not withholding necessary and efficacious medical care." Mechanic et al. (1995, 21–22) delineated three categories of managed care: prepaid health plans or health maintenance organizations, utilization management by third-party organizations, and high-cost case management.

Sunley (1997) further divided managed care into two distinct categories: insured programs, where services are provided through a panel of providers in their private offices, and HMOs, where services are usually provided in the HMO's physical plant by its own staff. Both insured and HMO mental

---

[1]Portions of this section are included in a published article: Bransford, C., & Bakken, T. (2002). The evolution of mental healthcare policy and the implications for social work. *Social Work in Mental Health*, 1 (1), 3–26.

health programs generally rely upon utilization review practices and pre-approval for specified numbers of sessions. HMOs, in distinction from fee-for-service or reimbursement-based insured programs, utilize a capitated, prospective form of billing. HMOs are attractive to purchasers, such as employers, because they assume all or most financial risks after the employer pays the HMO a predetermined, contracted amount of money per month for each employee.

Mental Healthcare Today for Special Needs Populations[2]

Mental health services for the chronically mentally ill and other special needs populations (such as the homeless, children and adolescents, older adults, those with alcohol and substance abuse disorders, or dual mental health/substance abuse disorders) are largely funded through Medicare and Medicaid. Increasingly, these services are being provided by managed care organizations, rather than by public human service organizations. The danger in these models is that private MCOs may find special needs patients undesirable to treat (Mechanic et al. 1995).

Often, private plans use a model of treatment that emphasizes preventive services and acute care in outpatient settings. They often are not suited adequately to address the needs of special populations, who typically require an array of specialized services. Also, private MCOs are not subject to the same legal regulations that govern human service organizations and, thus, they are not legally obliged or equipped to provide the same intricate web of services to special needs populations. Without safeguards, vulnerable persons may be underserved, and the ultimate social costs that are borne by families, the community, and the legal system may be staggering (Hurley & Draper 1998; Mechanic et al. 1995).

A number of states are now funneling their Medicaid recipients into managed care programs (McFarland 1996). Indeed, as of June 2002, more than 50% of Medicaid recipients were enrolled in private managed health-

---

[2]Portions of this section are included in a published article: Bransford, C., & Bakken, T. (2002). The evolution of mental healthcare policy and the implications for social work. *Social Work in Mental Health*, 1 (1), 3–26.

care plans (Centers for Medical and Medicaid Services 2007). Moreover, many persons with chronic and persistent mental illness receive Medicaid because of their status as Supplemental Security Income (SSI) recipients. Thus, a significant and increasing proportion of poor, publicly funded, disabled persons are receiving their mental health services under the auspices of private, managed healthcare plans. There is considerable question about whether the special needs of high risk chronically mentally ill persons will be served by a healthcare system that is primarily concerned with cost reduction and more generally equipped to deal with acute illnesses in medical model settings.

Moreover, the structure of Medicaid reimbursement policies may provide a disincentive for prepaid health plans to provide proper services for chronically mentally ill persons (Mechanic 1999). That is, Medicaid has more liberal reimbursement schedules for inpatient than outpatient care. The result may be that the care of poor persons may be limited to brief hospitalizations in psychiatric units of general hospitals when these persons may need more comprehensive services.

Mechanic (2001) noted that the length of inpatient hospitalizations stays for mental health and substance abuse treatment has been significantly reduced under managed care delivery systems and requests for extra inpatient days are much more likely to be denied than days for medical and surgical conditions. The lower status of mental healthcare within the healthcare system, coupled with the fact that utilization review practices may not distinguish between greater and lesser need when resources are being allocated (Mechanic & Alpine 1999), make the treatment of those with severe mental illness more vulnerable to excessive reductions in care.

Moreover, the lack of adequate community-based supports may compromise the ability of current mental health policies to meet the needs of vulnerable populations. Moreover, while not delivering comprehensive services, a fragmented social welfare system also makes data collection and outcome studies difficult for researchers to conduct, which further impedes the development of good public mental healthcare policies (Rothbard, Schinnar, Hadley, & Rovi 1990).

Some believe that the continued dependence of mental health policy on traditional health policy dooms it to failure (Kiesler 1992). Indeed, efforts to achieve mental health parity, which promotes the integration of health and mental healthcare, have been criticized by those who charge that integration efforts favor the mentally well (McFarland 1994). Moreover, efforts to reform healthcare may run the risk of obfuscating the need to develop comprehensive, integrated services for special needs populations, such as the severely mentally ill. Federal tax cuts totaling $2 trillion, during the period from 1980 to 1992, have resulted in major cuts in social programs and medical services. Thus, today there is inadequate public funding for mandated programs for special needs populations (Sunley 1997).

The Impact of Managed Care on Public Health

Of note, historically, there have been some apparent divisions between research emanating from the social casework literature and research generated from the field of public health. For example, much of social casework literature has tended to focus on the problems that social workers experience in grappling with issues pertaining to their professional identity vis-à-vis managed care practices (e.g., ethical concerns, confidentiality issues, decreased autonomy, etc.), as well as concerns about increased challenges in the provision of treatment to vulnerable populations under managed care guidelines. However, despite these concerns, comparisons between managed care systems of healthcare and fee-for-service plans have yielded mixed results. In fact, on some measures, managed care delivery systems have been found to be superior to traditional fee-for-service plans.

More recently, however, due to pressures from consumers for newer technologies and more provider choices, managed care health systems are becoming more expensive and arguably less effective, particularly for vulnerable populations. In order to attract more affluent subscribers, managed care plans are offering consumers more direct access to specialists and include point-of-service plans that allow enrollees to see out-of-network service providers. Such strategies result in higher premiums and are reducing some of the cost-savings advantages of managed care plans.

For example, Mechanic (2002, 459) has argued that indiscriminate referrals of patients to new, cutting edge medical screenings that involve the latest and most sophisticated technologies often lead patients on treatment trajectories that are "difficult to control and which result in many being labeled with diagnoses that they do not have and receiving interventions they do not need." Moreover, efforts to increase consumers' sophistication regarding the use of evidence-based medicine in decisions pertaining to their healthcare face significant barriers. Mechanic (2002, 459) suggests that those barriers "are the particular social and cultural influences on how people acquire and use information, the sources they trust and distrust, and the types of information they find credible and relevant to their situations."

In addition to driving up costs without necessarily improving the overall quality of healthcare, the subscriber groups that appear to suffer most under current managed care plans may indeed be the most vulnerable populations, including the poor, minorities, and the severely mentally ill (LaRoche & Turner 2002; Mechanic 2002). Furthermore, current public health research suggests that the proliferation of for-profit managed care plans is resulting in decreased quality care for persons with severe mental illness and other chronic health conditions (Himmelstein, Woolhandler, Hellender, & Wolfe 1999; Mechanic 1999, 2002; Mechanic & McAlpine 1999; Sullivan 1999).

LEVELS OF HEALTHCARE SERVICES

Cowles (2000) has identified three basic levels of healthcare services. These levels include primary care, which is focused on primary prevention and health maintenance; secondary care, which is focused on treating areas of health problems that have already emerged, with the goal of preventing worsening conditions; and tertiary care, which is focused on providing supportive and palliative care to persons whose health problems have advanced to the point of becoming chronic or terminal. Dhooper (1997) further delineates the areas of healthcare into four main sectors: acute care, ambulatory care, illness prevention and health promotion, and long-term care. Within these sectors, caseworkers and social workers provide services to a broad range of clients within a wide spectrum of settings.

Acute Care Settings

The primary setting for acute care services is the hospital. Emergency rooms, urgent care centers, intensive care units, newborn nurseries, and general medical and surgical departments are all examples of acute care settings. Psychiatric hospitals and nephrology or dialysis settings are other examples of acute care settings. According to Dhooper (1997), the primary special needs populations served by social workers in acute care settings include the elderly, persons with disabilities, persons with AIDS, and victims of domestic violence. Other specialized special needs populations may include those with severe and chronic mental illness, victims of natural and man-made disasters, and victims of community violence.

As Cowles (2000) has noted, the boundaries between practice settings have become increasingly blurred. For example, persons without health insurance or those whose access to traditional primary care settings are restricted may go to hospitals to receive their primary healthcare. Similarly, individuals who are recovering from acute health episodes or disabilities may find themselves treated in nursing homes. Both of these examples point to some of the current limitations in the accessibility and availability of appropriate healthcare within the current health system.

Primary Social Work Tasks in Acute Care Settings

The primary tasks for social workers involved in hospital work include case finding and access; discharge planning; involving the patient and family in planning; providing services that are timely and occur early in the hospitalization; and collaboration and teamwork.

▶ **Case Finding and Access**

This refers to the necessity of hospital social workers to identify patients within the hospital who may be in need of social work services. Cowles (2000, 141) identifies indicators that many hospitals use to screen patients for high social risk. These include anyone over the age of 65 and living alone, those with terminal or chronic illnesses, individuals with disabilities, those with disfiguring injuries or illnesses, victims of accidental injury, suicidal tendencies or attempts, those with developmental disabilities or mental health issues, extremely passive or aggressive behaviors, health problem related unemployment, low-income individuals, and unwed or minor mothers.

▶ **Discharge Planning**

Typically, the role of discharge planning involves the "arrangement of an appropriate follow-up service plan for return to a lesser level of care" (Dziegielewski 2004, 249).

In some cases, such as when working with elderly patients who are not able to return home, the plan may necessitate a greater level of aftercare. Discharge plans should be made in collaboration with the patient and the patient's family, and, as needed, with input from all helping professionals involved in the case. However, many social workers now feel that pressures from funding sources to limit hospitalization stays impedes their ability to do what they might believe is in the best interest of patients. This invariably creates ethical dilemmas and stress for hospital social workers, who may believe that patients are released into the community sooner than is optimal and without adequate supports in place.

▶ **Involving the Patient and Family in Planning**

Research has indicated that historically patients and their families were not adequately involved in discharge planning, to the detriment of later outcomes (Coulton 1990). In order to support patients' feeling a sense of control over the course of their medical treatment, Abrahmson (1990) recommended that "social workers offer choices to clients and explore rather than ignore signs of conflict between the key participants, continually advocating for the patients' right to control over decision making concerning their own lives" (as cited by Cowles 2000, 147–148).

▶ **The Importance of Teamwork and Collaboration**

The building of effective teamwork in hospital settings is crucial to the provision of comprehensive and holistic health-related services to patients. Yet, Dhooper (1997) points to the difficulty of achieving collaboration and teamwork among diverse professionals, who are used to operating in a culture that fosters competition, rather than cooperation. He suggests that by becoming aware of barriers to collaboration, more effective teamwork may result. For example, he suggests "fostering mechanisms for building, recognizing, and supporting interdependence" (1997, 147). Social workers may also need to display their expertise and willingness to help out by offering critical stress debriefing to hospital staff and psycho-educational trainings on how to reduce stress and other related issues. Some social work programs now have courses taken by typical professionals making up teams in order to socialize young professionals into cooperative team models.

Ambulatory Care Settings

Ambulatory care is one of the primary areas of social work practice in healthcare. The spiraling cost of healthcare and limits imposed by insurance companies on hospital stays ensure that systems of public health will increasingly move toward ambulatory care as the preferred setting of healthcare. Indeed, this is already occurring, as can be evidenced in the increase of outpatient surgical procedures, and the push to reduce hospitalization stays for both medical and mental health issues.

Ambulatory care settings include individual practices, group practices, hospital outpatient departments, public clinics, neighborhood health centers, ambulatory surgery centers, urgent care centers, and hospital emergency rooms. Other settings include community treatment centers, outpatient mental health centers, substance abuse centers, child and maternal health centers, and dialysis centers. Typical healthcare services provided in ambulatory settings include screening for diseases, immunizations and vaccinations, diagnostics, ongoing care, follow-up care, and specialized tests and procedures.

Caseworkers and social workers have been involved in many types of ambulatory settings, including "public health departments, health centers, health maintenance organizations, clinics for genetic counseling, family planning, pre-natal and post-natal care, care of the newborn, diagnostic and treatment management of persons with disabilities, service to those with AIDS, and work with victims of child abuse, rape, and spousal abuse" (Dhooper 1997, 173).

Primary Social Work Tasks in Ambulatory Care Settings
In ambulatory settings, social workers provide psychosocial assessments, coordination of care, integration of care, and patient-centered care that

living, health services, and a number of activities" (Care Pathways 2008, paragraph 2).

Dhoooper (1997, 85) identifies basic services provided by nursing homes: a) nursing care, which includes giving medications orally and intra-venously, tube feeding, wound care, physical, occupational, and speech therapy; b) personal care; c) residential services, including physical security of surroundings, supervision, and social services; and d) medical care, including visits by a medical doctor, special diets, and restorative and rehabilitative procedures.

Community Residential Care Settings

Community residential care settings include adult foster care homes, group homes, and adult homes for elderly persons and persons with mental illnesses. These programs were the outgrowth of the community mental health movement of the 1970s that began following the massive deinstitutionalization of mental health patients from state psychiatric hospitals.

Home-Based Care

Home-based care refers to services that are provided in a person's own home. These services are often provided and overseen by formal caregivers from health and human service organizations. The Older Americans Act provides funding for such services as congregate meal sites, senior citizens' centers, home care, and the Long Term Care Ombudsman Program, which, according the United States Senate Special Committee on Aging, plays a "key role in protecting the elderly and disabled. In every state, ombudsmen serve as advocates for patients, helping them resolve complaints of abuse, neglect, and mistreatment. Unfortunately, a lack of resources and staff make it difficult for the state ombudsman programs to serve the large number of people who require their services, leaving patients vulnerable to substandard care" (United States Senate Special Committee on Aging n.d., paragraph 1).

A recent report by the Institute of Medicine of the National Academy of Sciences, "Improving the Quality of Long-Term Care," noted the importance of routine, on-site presence of ombudspeople in detecting problems before they become serious. The report recommended "one ombudsman for every 2,000 nursing home residents" (United States Senate Special Committee on Aging n.d., paragraph 2).

Social Work Tasks in Long-Term Care Settings

Long-term care may consist of diagnostic, preventative, supportive, rehabilitative, habilitative, maintenance, and personal care services provided by specially trained or licensed professionals. Care may be provided in the home, in community-based programs, or in institutional settings. Social workers and caseworkers may work in a variety of roles in all of these settings, or may work in governmental departments or agencies that oversee, manage, and provide services and referrals to persons in long-term settings.

ILLNESS PREVENTION AND HEALTH PROMOTION

It is widely believed that within the next century, public health policy will focus its efforts more exclusively on the prevention of illness and the promotion of health than ever before in its history. Indeed, this paradigm shift is occurring already, as we see movement toward wellness and recovery models of health and mental healthcare, a focus on individual strengths and empowerment approaches, and collaborative models of provider-patient healthcare.

Dhooper draws a distinction between illness prevention and health promotion.

> "Health promotion is a pre-pathogenic level of intervention, whereas in disease prevention, the known agents or environmental factors are the focus of intervention with the aim of reducing the occurrence of a specific disease" (1997, 207).

Currently, a serious lack of resources are allocated to meet the rising costs of healthcare. The American Public Health Association, the oldest professional membership association of public healthcare professionals with over 50,000 members from 50 different public health occupations, focuses its advocacy efforts in three primary areas: rebuilding the public health infrastructure, ensuring access to healthcare, and eliminating disparities in access to healthcare. The overview of their mission is as follows:

"APHA, in coordination with its members and state affiliates, works with key decision-makers to shape public policy to address today's ongoing public health concerns such as ensuring access to care, protecting funding for core public health programs and services and eliminating health disparities. APHA is also working to address emerging public health issues including pandemic flu preparedness, children's health, access to care, environmental health, managed care, public health infrastructure, disease control, health disparities, bioterrorism, international health and tobacco control" (American Public Health Association n.d., b, paragraph 2).

In addition to allocating more federal and state funds toward preventative healthcare, there is also a need to plan for community-wide health education programs, enforced regulation of industries that pollute the environment and cause undue risks to public health, and greater efforts at risk-reduction interventions, such as programs to reduce smoking and promote healthy weight and exercise.

Specialized areas of social work practice within illness prevention and health promotion include AIDS and hepatitis C prevention, child abuse prevention, and health promotion and illness prevention among aging adults.

HEALTH POLICY ISSUES

A number of specialized areas of public health policy are likely to present current and continuing challenges to social workers employed within public health agencies. These areas include AIDS prevention, child abuse prevention, and geriatric health promotion (Dhooper 1997). Other issues that are likely to be the focus of public health policy efforts include community violence, disaster preparedness, obesity prevention, and alcohol and drug abuse prevention. Although it will be impossible to cover all of these areas in depth within this chapter, I will review several of those that continue to present the biggest challenges to caseworkers and social workers operating within public health contexts.

HIV and AIDS

Social workers have been at the forefront of efforts to support individuals living with HIV and AIDS since it first became recognized as an epidemic in the 1980s. The human immunodeficiency virus (HIV) causes an infection in the body that, left untreated, can lead to acquired immunodeficiency syndrome (AIDS). AIDS is a disease that affects the immune system, causing the body to become susceptible to rare and often fatal diseases.

The World Health Organization offers the following definition and description of HIV/AIDS:

> The human immunodeficiency virus (HIV) is a retrovirus that infects cells of the human immune system, destroying or impairing their function. In the early stages of infection, the person has no symptoms. However, as the infection progresses, the immune system becomes weaker, and the person becomes more susceptible to so-called opportunistic infections.
>
> The most advanced stage of HIV infection is acquired immunodeficiency syndrome (AIDS). It can take 10–15 years for an HIV-infected person to develop AIDS; antiretroviral drugs can slow down the process even further.
>
> HIV is transmitted through unprotected sexual intercourse (oral, anal, or vaginal), transfusion of contaminated blood, sharing of contaminated needles, and between a mother and her infant during pregnancy, childbirth and breastfeeding (World Health Organization n.d., paragraphs 1–3).

At the beginning of the epidemic, people coping with AIDS faced a great deal of discrimination from many in the population who considered it to be a homosexual disease, thus slowing the response of federal, state, and local governments to develop preventative treatment (NASW 2006). Indeed, AIDS does affect primarily disempowered groups, such as gay and bisexual men, women and men of color, and IV drug users in the United States. However, worldwide, HIV/AIDS is found among heterosexuals.

Recent advances in treatment and wider distribution of antiviral drugs have also made it possible for people with HIV to live longer. The advances in medical science, however, have had the unintended consequence of inducing at-risk people to take greater risks, thinking that if they were to get infected, the antiviral drugs would minimize the consequences. Thus, the role for continued preventive education remains paramount.

The Joint United Nations Program on HIV/AIDS and World Health Organization (WHO 2007) estimate that in 2007, 33.2 million people were living with HIV, 2.5 million people became newly infected, and 2.1 million people died of AIDS. Global HIV incidence—the number of new HIV infections per year—is now estimated to have peaked in the late 1990s at over 3 million new infections per year, and is estimated in 2007 to be 2.5 million new infections, an average of more than 6,800 new infections each day. While the overall rates of global HIV infection have leveled off, the numbers of people infected with the virus have increased due to ongoing acquisition of the virus, people living longer with the virus, and the increasing population rate.

The Council of State Governments offers the following information about AIDS:

> HIV/AIDS continues to hit minorities, particularly African-Americans, the hardest. Although African-Americans make up just 13 percent of the U.S. population, they accounted for half of the new diagnoses of HIV/AIDS in 2004. Forty percent of all AIDS cases since the beginning of the epidemic are African-Americans, and once infected, they do not live as long as people in other racial or ethnic groups.
>
> Young people (13 to 24 years old) also are at a particularly high risk of contracting HIV. In 2004, an estimated 5,000 young people received a new diagnosis of HIV/AIDS, which was 13% of all new diagnoses that year.
>
> Policymakers can help fight HIV/AIDS infections through a variety of ways, including:
>
> ▶ Reducing barriers that prevent people from getting tested, such as written consent requirements before testing;

▶ Supporting efforts to make HIV testing a routine part of medical care, such as anti-stigma campaigns and working closely with healthcare providers to stress the importance of testing;

▶ Requiring the use of confidential, name-based reporting of all HIV infections; and

▶ Working locally to keep HIV/AIDS on the state's public health agenda (The Council of State Governments 2004).

Disability Issues

One out of every three people will acquire a disability within his or her lifetime. Disabilities may be defined broadly and include physical, sensory, and cognitive impairments, as well as mental, physical, and chronic illnesses. Disabilities often cause functional impairments. Some disabilities are apparent, others are not. Although some disabilities are temporary, many last a lifetime (NASW 2001). Thus, individuals with disabilities comprise a large proportion of the caseloads of social workers.

For many years, people with disabilities were ostracized from their communities, either forced to live an isolated existence with family members or simply warehoused in institutions. Over the last 35 years, the public has become more sensitive to the needs of people with disabilities, who are now beginning to lead more satisfying lives, integrating more fully within the communities within which they live. A number of laws have been passed to protect the rights of disabled persons, including the 1963 Mental Retardation Facilities and Community Mental Health Constructions Act, the Architectural Barriers Act of 1968, the Education of Handicapped Children Act and Individuals with Disabilities Education Act, both of 1975, and the Mental Health Bill of Rights Act of 1985.

Although these laws extended the legal rights and protections of individuals with disabilities, a common limitation was that these regulations often offered protection only with regard to governmental activities and programs. The passage of the Americans with Disabilities Act of 1990 changed all that and, for the first time, the law of the land mandated that persons with disabilities should be given legal rights within all segments of American society.

The Americans with Disabilities Act

The Americans with Disabilities Act, signed into law by President George H. W. Bush in 1990, provides legal protections to individuals with disabilities. The Job Accommodation Network, an online referral source sponsored by the United States Department of Labor, provides the following overview of the Act:

> Signed into law on July 26, 1990, the Americans with Disabilities Act is a wide-ranging legislation intended to make American Society more accessible to people with disabilities.
>
> It is divided into five titles:
>
> 1. **Employment (Title I)** Business must provide reasonable accommodations to protect the rights of individuals with disabilities in all aspects of employment. Possible changes may include restructuring jobs, altering the layout of workstations, or modifying equipment. Employment aspects may include the application process, hiring, wages, benefits, and all other aspects of employment. Medical examinations are highly regulated.
>
> 2. **Public Services (Title II)** Public services, which include state and local government instrumentalities, the National Railroad Passenger Corporation, and other commuter authorities, cannot deny services to people with disabilities participation in programs or activities which are available to people without disabilities. In addition, public transportation systems, such as public transit buses, must be accessible to individuals with disabilities.
>
> 3. **Public Accommodations (Title III)** All new construction and modifications must be accessible to individuals with disabilities. For existing facilities, barriers to services must be removed if readily achievable. Public accommodations include facilities such as restaurants, hotels, grocery stores, retail stores, etc., as well as privately owned transportation systems.
>
> 4. **Telecommunications (Title IV)** Telecommunications companies offering telephone service to the general public must have telephone relay service to individuals who use telecommunication devices for the deaf (TTYs) or similar devices.

5. **Miscellaneous (Title V)** Includes a provision prohibiting either (a) coercing or threatening or (b) retaliating against the disabled or those attempting to aid people with disabilities in asserting their rights under the ADA.

The ADA's protection applies primarily, but not exclusively, to "disabled" individuals. An individual is "disabled" if he or she meets at least any one of the following tests:

1. He or she has a physical or mental impairment that substantially limits one or more of his or her major life activities;
2. He or she has a record of such an impairment; or
3. He or she is regarded as having such an impairment.

Other individuals who are protected in certain circumstances include 1) those, such as parents, who have an association with an individual known to have a disability, and 2) those who are coerced or subjected to retaliation for assisting people with disabilities in asserting their rights under the ADA.

While the employment provisions of the ADA apply to employers of fifteen employees or more, its public accommodations provisions apply to all sizes of business, regardless of number of employees. State and local governments are covered regardless of size (Job Accommodation Network 1997).

Social Work Practice and Disabilities

Within the field of public health, caseworkers/social workers may obtain governmental positions as disability specialists or disability assistants. Within these jobs, caseworkers may determine individuals' eligibility for Social Security Disability (SSD) and/or Supplemental Security Income. They may also assist individuals with referrals to occupational rehabilitation programs, independent living, housing, and transportation services. They may ensure that people with disabilities receive specialized services, in-home care, and environmental modifications. Caseworkers may also assist persons with disabilities to obtain education and training so that they may become employable. They may also provide counseling and other forms of support to individuals with disabilities.

Caseworkers and social workers working in disabilities may be employed in a range of settings, from working in local public health departments, to working in developmental disability centers, agencies that offer specific services to vision-impaired individuals, and programs that provide services to persons with mental illness and mental retardation.

PUBLIC CHILD WELFARE

Public child welfare services include an array of services to promote the safety and welfare of children and families. These services enact society's mandate to protect and care for children. These services are both directly provided by public child welfare agencies and also contracted to private agencies. Services for children and families are typically classified in the following categories: preventative and supportive services, protective services, foster care services, and adoption services.

The latter three services—protective services, foster care services and adoption services—comprise the domain of child welfare. These services may be funded through the public sector, voluntary family and child agencies, or agencies founded under religious auspices. Some services are contracted to private, for-profit agencies.

- ▶ **Preventative Services** are designed to support families so that children are able to stay in their homes. This support may include concrete services, such as childcare, healthcare, food assistance, and transportation, or the provision of counseling and therapy to parents and children. Typically, a family must have a child under the age of 18 living in the home in order to qualify for preventative services.
- ▶ **Protective Services** are implemented once it has been determined that a child's basic care falls below a certain standard. For example, children have been found to be neglected or abused. Professional services are then provided in order to prevent placement of children into foster care or other residential programs.
- ▶ **Foster Care Services** are provided when a family can no longer maintain the child in the family home. When a child is placed in

foster care, the family is offered help so that the child may eventually return to the family. Children may be placed with relatives, also known as kinship care, or in group homes or residential treatment facilities, depending upon the level of structure that the child requires.

▶ **Adoption Services** are instituted when the parental rights are terminated, or when parents place their children for adoption. Older children are helped to grieve the loss of their biological families, and support is given to both the adoptive family and the biological family.

Definitions of Child Abuse and Neglect

The Child Abuse Prevention and Treatment Act of 1974 provided a national definition of child maltreatment:

Child abuse and neglect is, at a minimum:

▶ Any recent act or failure to act on the part of a parent or caretaker which results in death, serious physical or emotional harm, sexual abuse or exploitation; or

▶ Any act or failure to act which presents an imminent risk of serious harm.

Child Abuse and Neglect Fatalities

Children under the age of three are the most frequent victims of child fatalities. (See sidebar for child abuse and neglect fatalities, by age.) They are the most vulnerable, due to their dependency and inability to defend themselves. According to the Child Welfare Information Gateway's website:

"Fatal child abuse may involve repeated abuse over a period of time (e.g., battered child syndrome), or it may involve a single, impulsive incident (e.g., drowning, suffocating, or shaking a baby). In cases of fatal neglect, the child's death results not from anything the caregiver does, but from a caregiver's failure to act. The neglect may be chronic (e.g., extended malnourishment) or acute (e.g., an infant who drowns after being left unsupervised in the bathtub)" (Child Welfare Information Gateway 2006).

Shaken Baby Syndrome

According to the Child Welfare Information Gateway, Shaken Baby Syndrome (SBS) is defined as "the collection of signs and symptoms resulting from the violent shaking of an infant or small child" (n.d., a, paragraph 1). The violent shaking of an infant causes neurological damage and often leads to death.

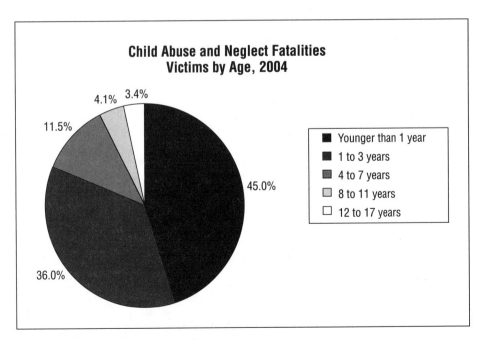

Source: Child Welfare Information Gateway, 2006.

The National Center on Shaken Baby Syndrome offers the following information about SBS on its website:

> "Shaken baby syndrome (SBS) is the leading cause of death in abusive head trauma cases. An estimated 1,200 to 1,400 children are injured or killed by shaking every year in the United States. Actual numbers may be much higher as many likely go undetected.
>
> Approximately 25% of all SBS victims die as a result of their injuries. Victims who survive may suffer permanent disability such as severe brain damage, cerebral palsy, mental retardation, behavioral disorders and impaired motor and cognitive skills. Many survivors require constant medical or personal attention, which places tremendous emotional and financial strain on families. Medical costs associated with initial and long-term care for these children can range from $300,000 to more than $1,000,000" (n.d., a, paragraphs 3–4).

The National Center on Shaken Baby Syndrome lists the following common symptoms of SBS:

- ▶ lethargy/decreased muscle tone
- ▶ extreme irritability
- ▶ decreased appetite, poor feeding or vomiting for no apparent reason
- ▶ no smiling or vocalizations
- ▶ poor sucking or swallowing
- ▶ rigidity or posturing
- ▶ difficulty breathing
- ▶ seizures
- ▶ head or forehead appears larger than usual or soft-spot on head appears to be bulging
- ▶ inability to lift head
- ▶ inability of eyes to focus or track movement or unequal size of pupils (n.d., b, paragraph 3).

Human service professionals are required by law to report suspected cases of Shaken Baby Syndrome to the child abuse and neglect hotline.

Mandated Reporting

The 1974 Child Abuse Prevention and Treatment Act requires reporting of suspected child abuse in all 50 states and the District of Columbia. Mandated reporters include all physicians and other medical personnel, mental health professionals, social workers, teachers, school officials, childcare workers, and law enforcement personnel. As of 2000, 18 states require all citizens to report, and all states allow any citizen to report. Those required by law to report suspected child maltreatment are called "mandated reporters" (NASW 2006).

Despite the major improvement in the reporting of suspected child maltreatment, two major problems continue to occur. A large number of cases continue to go unreported, and there are many unfounded reports. Indeed, 60% of all reported cases are found, on investigation, to be without enough basis to warrant further action. Some of these are made by citizens who may not know the definitions of child maltreatment, and others are made by people involved in child custody disputes. Still another reason for unfounded reports may be due to insufficiently trained child protective workers, who may not recognize when actual child maltreatment is occurring. However, of the cases not substantiated on the first investigation, many are re-reported and found to meet child abuse and neglect criteria. There is a growing awareness that many of the cases that do not meet legal requirements would benefit from services, and many are referred for services (e.g., parenting classes or counseling) referred to as "alternative response."

New workers often consult first with their supervisors to discuss suspected abuse or neglect and to find out whether or not the abuse should be reported. However, there is no choice about reporting the abuse. If you are aware of abuse and have discussed it with your supervisor, document that discussion in the record. Some states will revoke a professional's license if abuse is not reported. Social workers can be sanctioned by the state NASW ethics committee, and membership in NASW can be revoked.

Signs of Child Maltreatment

The Child Welfare Information Gateway (CWIG 2006) has issued the following information on how to recognize signs and symptoms of child abuse and neglect:

> The first step in helping abused or neglected children is learning to recognize the signs of child abuse and neglect. The presence of a single sign does not prove child abuse is occurring in a family; however, when these signs appear repeatedly or in combination you should take a closer look at the situation and consider the possibility of child abuse.
>
> If you do suspect a child is being harmed, reporting your suspicions may protect the child and get help for the family. Contact your local child protective services agency or police department.

Recognizing Child Abuse

The Child Welfare Information Gateway has also provided a list of the signs of child abuse or neglect:

The child:
▶ shows sudden changes in behavior or school performance.
▶ has not received help for physical or medical problems brought to the parents' attention.
▶ has learning problems (or difficulty concentrating) that cannot be attributed to specific physical or psychological causes.
▶ is always watchful, as though preparing for something bad to happen.
▶ lacks adult supervision.
▶ is overly compliant, passive, or withdrawn.
▶ comes to school or other activities early, stays late, and does not want to go home.

The parent:
▶ shows little concern for the child.
▶ denies the existence of—or blames the child for—the child's problems in school or at home.

- ► asks teachers or other caretakers to use harsh physical discipline if the child misbehaves.
- ► sees the child as entirely bad, worthless, or burdensome.
- ► demands a level of physical or academic performance the child cannot achieve.
- ► looks primarily to the child for care, attention, and satisfaction of emotional needs.

The parent and child:

- ► rarely touch or look at each other.
- ► consider their relationship entirely negative.
- ► state that they do not like each other.

Types of Abuse

The Child Welfare Information Gateway has also noted signs associated with particular types of child abuse and neglect, including physical abuse, neglect, sexual abuse, and emotional abuse. They note, however, that these types of abuse are more typically found in combination with one another, rather than alone. For example, a physically abused child may often also be emotionally abused; a sexually abused child may also be neglected. The CWIG offers the following signs of physical abuse, neglect, sexual abuse, and emotional maltreatment:

Signs of Physical Abuse

Consider the possibility of physical abuse when the **child**:

- ► has unexplained burns, bites, bruises, broken bones, or black eyes.
- ► has fading bruises or other marks noticeable after an absence from school.
- ► seems frightened of the parents and protests or cries when it is time to go home.
- ► shrinks at the approach of adults.
- ► reports injury by a parent or another adult caregiver.

Consider the possibility of physical abuse when the **parent or other adult caregiver**:

- ► offers conflicting, unconvincing, or no explanation for the child's injury.

▶ describes the child as "evil," or in some other very negative way.

▶ uses harsh physical discipline with the child.

▶ has a history of abuse as a child.

Signs of Neglect

Consider the possibility of neglect when the **child**:

▶ is frequently absent from school.

▶ begs or steals food or money.

▶ lacks needed medical or dental care, immunizations, or glasses.

▶ is consistently dirty and has severe body odor.

▶ lacks sufficient clothing for the weather.

▶ abuses alcohol or other drugs.

▶ states that there is no one at home to provide care.

Consider the possibility of neglect when the **parent or other adult caregiver**:

▶ appears to be indifferent to the child.

▶ seems apathetic or depressed.

▶ behaves irrationally or in a bizarre manner.

▶ is abusing alcohol or other drugs.

Signs of Sexual Abuse

Consider the possibility of sexual abuse when the **child**:

▶ has difficulty walking or sitting.

▶ suddenly refuses to change for gym or to participate in physical activities.

▶ reports nightmares or bed-wetting.

▶ experiences a sudden change in appetite.

▶ demonstrates bizarre, sophisticated, or unusual sexual knowledge or behavior.

▶ becomes pregnant or contracts a venereal disease, particularly if under age 14.

▶ runs away.

▶ reports sexual abuse by a parent or another adult caregiver.

Consider the possibility of sexual abuse when the **parent or other adult caregiver**:

▶ is unduly protective of the child or severely limits the child's contact with other children, especially of the opposite sex.

▶ is secretive and isolated.

▶ is jealous or controlling with family members.

Signs of Emotional Maltreatment

Consider the possibility of emotional maltreatment when the **child**:

▶ shows extremes in behavior, such as overly compliant or demanding behavior, extreme passivity, or aggression.

▶ is either inappropriately adult (parenting other children, for example) or inappropriately infantile (frequently rocking or head-banging, for example).

▶ is delayed in physical or emotional development.

▶ has attempted suicide.

▶ reports a lack of attachment to the parent.

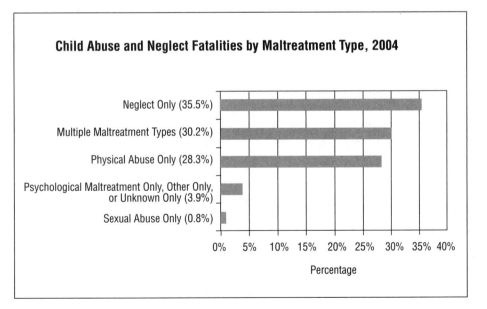

Child Abuse and Neglect Fatalities by Maltreatment Type, 2004

Source: Child Welfare Information Gateway, 2006.

Consider the possibility of emotional maltreatment when the **parent or other adult caregiver**:

▶ constantly blames, belittles, or berates the child.

▶ is unconcerned about the child and refuses to consider offers of help for the child's problems.

▶ overtly rejects the child (Child Welfare Information Gateway 2006).

Preventative Services

Research has shown that episodes of child abuse and neglect may be avoided if families are provided with support and services. These findings have led to more and better services to protect children in their own homes from abuse and neglect. Preventative services and family support services are programs that have been developed to prevent abuse and neglect and strengthen family functioning. Your state's Children's Trust Fund can offer important information about preventative services.

Downs, Moore, McFadden, Michaud, and Costin (2004, 92) have defined preventative services as "any program that has as its main goal the prevention of child maltreatment"; and family support services as a "type of preventative program specifically intended to support family functioning."

Bloom (1996) has defined prevention as "coordinated actions seeking to prevent predictable problems, to protect existing states of health and health functioning, and to promote desired potentialities in individuals and groups in their physical and sociocultural settings over time" (p. 2, as quoted by Downs et al. 2004). At their best, preventative services are designed to support families and communities so that they, in turn, may be better prepared to adequately support and sustain the healthy development of children and the effective social functioning of all family members. Program components include psycho-education of parents about child development and parenting skills, parent-child and group activities, crisis intervention, and information and referral services.

Family Support Services

The Family Preservation and Support Services Act of 1993 addressed the need for family support services, which are services designed to support both families and communities. The Act both provided voluntary services to support family functioning, and also mandated services for families who already had abused or neglected their children and were in need of more intensive services in order to preserve their families and prevent foster care.

Examples of family support service programs include Healthy Families America, which provides in-home visits for parents and their newborns; family support programs for teen parents; special services for pregnant and parenting teens; and family support programs for economically deprived communities. A range of services are available within these programs including therapeutic services, provided by licensed clinical social workers, casework with parents, individual and group work with children, and family therapy. These programs are all targeted to both parents and their children (Downs et al. 2004).

Prevention Programs for Children and Adolescents

Preventative services geared specifically to children and adolescents include sexual abuse prevention programs, teenage pregnancy prevention programs, sex education programs, and youth development programs. All of these services offer job opportunities for caseworkers.

Protective Services

Once a report of suspected abuse or neglect is filed, an investigation is conducted by caseworkers employed by the department of social services or police department. In some states, local police departments are taking on a much greater role because of the need for social workers to provide services to families. If the allegations are substantiated, the family may be referred for counseling and other associated concrete services, such as food stamps or other social services. If it is determined that the child is not safe remaining in the home, then the child may be referred to protective services. At this juncture in the child welfare system, the child may be placed with foster services such as a diagnostic facility or group home, a foster family, or a suitable family member.

Britain and Hunt define child protective services, or CPS, as "specialized supports and interventions for neglected, abused, or exploited children and their families" (2004, 50). The authors further explain that the intent of CPS workers is to "focus on rehabilitating the family and home through interventions and services that address the specific situations and conditions that lead to child maltreatment. The term family is used broadly, and persons within a family should make the designation of who to include in the family unit" (2004, 50).

Responsibilities of the Child Protective Services Caseworker

The responsibilities of the CPS caseworker include the following:

- ▶ Determine the immediate safety of the child and risk for potential harm.
- ▶ Determine if abuse or neglect has occurred.
- ▶ Assess the strengths and needs of the target child and family to identify the issues and risks.
- ▶ Determine the need for services.
- ▶ Provide direct services to strengthen families and protect children.
- ▶ Coordinate community services.
- ▶ Seek family involvement in case decisions while drawing on the knowledge and expertise of a multidisciplinary team of professionals.
- ▶ Be culturally responsive when assessing and serving families of various backgrounds (Britain and Hunt 2004, 53).

Child protective services workers' roles include those of evaluator, court room testifier, case manager, collaborators, therapeutic treatment provider, advocate, administrator, and supervisor.

Foster Care

The Adoption and Safe Families Act of 1997 was passed in order to address the problem of too many children remaining in foster care for too long, without any chance of returning home to their families, and without any alternate permanent plan in place. In 2000, nearly a third of children in foster care had been there for three years or more. Almost one-fourth of the children in foster care were identified as unlikely to ever return to their biological families. Currently, the law expedites procedures and requires states to file for permanent termination of parental rights for any child in foster care for 15 of the most recent 22 months, unless the child is living with a relative or there is a compelling mitigating reason (Downs et al. 2004).

Foster care includes the following basic characteristics:

1. It is arranged by a public; private nonprofit; or private for-profit social agency.
2. Responsibility for children's daily care usually is transferred from the biological parents because of a serious situation.
3. Foster care is full time care, 24 hours a day, outside the child's own home.
4. Foster care or out-of-home care may be given within a relative's home, a nonrelated-family foster home, a treatment foster home, a small group home, a cottage setting, a larger residential care facility, or, if the child is old enough, in his or her own residence with independent living program supervision.
5. In contrast with adoption, foster care is a temporary arrangement, with the expectation that the child will return to the parents or extended family, be placed for adoption, or be discharged from care on reaching legal maturity (Downs et al. 2004, 323).

Adoption

Adoption may be defined as "a social and legal process whereby the parent-child relationship is established between persons not so related by birth" (Downs et al. 2004, 366).

In the early twentieth century, most formal adoption services attempted to match healthy white infants with upwardly mobile upper-middle class and upper class families. However, the numbers of healthy white infants available for adoption began to decrease in the 1970s, primarily due to increased use of birth control, the legalization of abortion, and the lessened stigma of single mothers keeping their infants, and also due to the advent of child abuse reporting laws, and the influx of children into the child welfare system who later become released for adoption. Potential adoptive parents moved in the direction of adopting older children, children with special needs, children from multiracial backgrounds, and children born outside the United States.

Moreover, conventional definitions of family have expanded to include people who might not have previously been considered suitable parents. Now, gay and lesbian individuals and couples, people with AIDS, single adults, and senior citizens are becoming adoptive parents. Also, children who were previously considered to be unadoptable, such as children with disabilities, emotional difficulties, cognitive impairments, or medical conditions and older children, are increasingly being released for adoption—often because they have become subsidized guardianship by the state either in monthly cash payments or medical coverage. Nonetheless, thousands of children and adolescents continue to linger in the foster care system waiting for a permanent home.

The role of the biological parents is also changing. The advent of open adoptions has made a greater role for biological parents in the lives of their adopted offspring, often remaining in their biological child's life through the child's development.

CHILD AND ADOLESCENT SERVICE SYSTEM PROGRAM (SYSTEMS OF CARE)

In 1984, the National Institute of Mental Health (NIMH) established a program called the Child and Adolescent Service System Program (CASSP). Today, the U.S. Department of Health and Human Services provides technical support and disperses a budget of over $10 million dollars to all 50 states to provide CASSP services, also known as "Systems of Care," to children with emotional disorders. This program seeks to redress the lack of coordination and comprehensiveness of services for children and adolescents with mental disorders.

The CASSP concept facilitates cross-system collaboration among a range of systems of care that deal with children. These systems of care include family, school, social service agencies, medical facilities, juvenile justice services, substance abuse services, child welfare, recreational systems, or vocational services. An interagency approach is mandated under this program, thus diffusing turf wars among agencies (Summers 2006).

Caseworkers and case managers working with CASSP value the primary role of the family and facilitate collaborative relationships with families and agencies in planning, monitoring, and evaluating services. The caseworkers and case managers identify naturally occurring community resources that may be made available to the family, such as religious, extended family, and other social supports. Services should take place in settings that are the least restrictive and intrusive as possible to meet the needs of the child and family. Also, caseworkers and case managers should be culturally competent when working with children and families from diverse backgrounds.

CHILD AND ADOLESCENT MENTAL HEALTH

All helping professionals who provide direct or case management services to children and their families need to be aware of the kinds of mental health issues that children may be facing. In this section, we will begin to examine some of the common problems that children may have and the *Diagnostic and Statistical Manual of Mental Disorders*, Fourth Edition, Text Revised Edition (DSM IV-TR) criteria for diagnosing them.

Attention Deficit/Hyperactivity Disorder

Attention Deficit/Hyperactivity Disorder (ADHD) is characterized by difficulty remaining focused on activities and sitting still. The diagnosis is made by examining both the child's level of hyperactivity and impulsivity, and also the child's level of inattention. Many children receive a diagnosis of Attention Deficit/Hyperactivity Disorder. Frequently, children who are diagnosed with this condition are placed on medications, such as Ritalin, a stimulant medication that increases the amount of dopamine in the blood. Dopamine creates alertness in people, leading to focused, purposeful behavior. SSRIs are also used to treat ADHD. Effective interventions include medical, special education, and parenting psycho-education and counseling. A great deal of controversy exists as to whether children are overdiagnosed with ADHD and unnecessarily placed on medication. For example, some parents view the problem as related to the excessive rigidity in which classrooms are structured, or diet, rather than existing within the child. Nonetheless, medication and behavioral treatment techniques are frequently successful in alleviating the symptoms of ADHD and improving learning and behavior.

The National Institute of Mental Health (NIMH) has defined ADHD as:

> a condition that becomes apparent in some children in the preschool and early school years. It is hard for these children to control their behavior and/or pay attention. It is estimated that between 3 and 5 percent of children have ADHD, or approximately 2 million children in the United States. This means that in a classroom of 25 to 30 children, it is likely that at least one will have ADHD (NIMH 2007, paragraph 1).

Oppositional Defiant Disorder

Children with oppositional defiant disorder (ODD) will exhibit the following behaviors: frequent temper tantrums, defying authority figures, appearing hostile, refusing to carry out simple requests, blaming others for their difficulties, deliberately annoying others, frequent anger and resentment, and seeking revenge. Children with this diagnosis may be responding to a combination of biological and environmental factors, and can benefit from a combination of behavioral interventions and parental counseling. They may need to find more appropriate avenues for expression of their anger and disappointment.

The American Academy of Child and Adolescent Psychiatry (1999) estimates that between 5 and 15% of all school-aged children may suffer from ODD. They also suggest the following treatment for ODD: parent training programs to help the parent manage their child's behavior, psychotherapy to help the child develop anger management skills, family therapy to address communication problems, cognitive-behavior therapy to assist with problem solving and decrease negativity, and social skills training.

Conduct Disorder

Children with conduct disorder typically present with a pattern of antisocial behavior such as bullying, fighting, physically or sexually assaulting others, torturing animals, vandalism, setting fires, breaking windows, and theft. These children may also run away from home and become involved in prostitution or selling drugs. Frequently, these children are truant from school resulting in expulsion. They may be arrested and sentenced to youth detention centers. Some professionals believe that a diagnosis of conduct disorder in childhood may lead to the development of antisocial personality disorder.

Effective interventions in treating conduct disorder may include behavior therapy and dynamic psychotherapy to help the child to both control and also express anger. Some children are in need of special education. Parents may need to be coached in behavioral contingency methods. Medication may also be used in some children, particularly those with attention difficulties, impulsivity, or depression.

Separation Anxiety Disorder

Older children and adolescents who experience excessive amounts of anxiety at separation from attachment figures may be diagnosed with separation anxiety disorder. These children often fear that something untoward will befall their loved one when they are separated. For example, they may fear that the attachment figure may be hit by lightning or become poisoned.

Some children who suffer from this disorder may refuse to go to school, or find it impossible to attend sleepovers or other functions that keep them away from home. They may become psychosomatic, complaining of physical ailments in order to stay home with attachment figures. These symptoms interfere with the child's social, academic, or occupational functioning.

Generalized Anxiety Disorder

Children who worry unrealistically about their academic performance, athletic abilities, and being on time, and constantly seek reassurance and approval from adults, may be considered for a diagnosis of Generalized Anxiety Disorder (GAD). Often these children are perfectionists, and do well academically. Typically, they have not experienced any overt trauma or catastrophe in their past. Symptoms include restlessness or feeling on edge, fatigue, difficulty concentrating, irritability, muscle tension, stomachaches, and sleep disturbance. The mean age for onset is 8 years old. Treatment for GAD includes cognitive-behavioral therapy and family anxiety management training, where parents are taught to reinforce their children's courageous behaviors and model positive responses to anxiety-provoking events.

Post-Traumatic Stress Disorder

Children and adolescents who have experienced a traumatic event in their lives, such as sexual or physical abuse, automobile accident, or sudden death of parents or other close relatives, are at risk for developing post-traumatic stress disorder (PTSD). Symptoms include intrusive and recurrent memories of the event, flashbacks or dissociative episodes, dreams of the event, extreme stress when exposed to situations that evoke memories of the event, and nightmares. Children may become involved in repetitive play where themes or elements of the event are re-enacted. Treatment includes psychotherapy, where the child gains a sense of mastery over the event. Younger children may be helped through play therapy, where they are able to process and master the past event. Relaxation training and supportive psychotherapy may also be helpful.

Reactive Attachment Disorder

Reactive attachment disorder is a disturbance in social relationships caused by early childhood neglect. Babies placed in orphanages who have been raised by multiple caregivers are at risk for developing this disorder. The disorder is caused by a neglect of an infant's needs for touching, physical safety, emotional bonding, and nourishment. Causes include parental isolation, teen parents, and inadequate parental skills.

A child with reactive attachment disorder may exhibit symptoms that include recoiling from social interactions, isolation, impaired ability to be comforted or to self-soothe, and avoidance of physical contact. Children with reactive attachment disorder may also be indiscriminately sociable with strangers, putting them at risk for sexual abuse.

Treatment includes ensuring that the child is in a safe environment, and offering parenting skills training to the caregivers. If necessary, counseling may also be offered to the parent to address any potential complicating issues, such as drug abuse or dependence.

Substance Abuse

The National Survey on Research and Health indicates that some children are already abusing drugs at age 12 or 13, or even earlier. According to the National Institute of Drug Abuse (NIDA), "early childhood abuse often includes the use of tobacco, alcohol, inhalants, marijuana, and prescription drugs, such as sleeping pills and anti-anxiety medicines. If drug abuse persists into later adolescence, abusers typically become more heavily involved with marijuana and then advance to other drugs, while continuing their abuse of tobacco and alcohol" (n.d., paragraph 16).

Adolescents are at the highest risk for using alcohol and drugs on a consistent basis. Often, these substances are used to self-medicate for depression or early schizophrenia. Adolescents also experience increased stress due to pressure to perform well academically. Adolescents may also receive less supervision and/or inconsistent attention from the parents, due to the increase in single parents and dual wage earning parents. Symptoms may include school failure, change in attitude, irritability, and withdrawal. Caseworkers should screen carefully for substance use when doing a social history. Children and adolescents with substance abuse problems should be referred for substance abuse treatment. Parental skills training can also be effective in treating substance abuse in children and adolescents.

Depression

The rates of depression among children and adolescents have increased dramatically over the last few years. The American Academy of Child and Adolescent Psychiatry (AACAP) estimates that about 5% of all children and adolescents suffer from depression. Children who are experiencing stress or loss, or who have an attention, learning, conduct, or anxiety disorder are at greater risk for developing depression. There is also a genetic predisposition to developing depression. A history of depression in a family member is a risk factor for depression.

The AACAP has identified the following list of signs and symptoms of depression in children and adolescents:

- ▶ frequent sadness, tearfulness, crying
- ▶ hopelessness
- ▶ decreased interest in activities; or inability to enjoy previously favorite activities
- ▶ persistent boredom; low energy
- ▶ social isolation, poor communication
- ▶ low self-esteem and guilt
- ▶ extreme sensitivity to rejection or failure
- ▶ increased irritability, anger, or hostility
- ▶ difficulty with relationships
- ▶ frequent complaints of physical illnesses such as headaches and stomachaches
- ▶ frequent absences from school or poor performance in school
- ▶ poor concentration
- ▶ a major change in eating and/or sleeping patterns
- ▶ talk of or efforts to run away from home
- ▶ thoughts or expressions of suicide or self-destructive behavior (AACAP 2004, paragraph 4)

Recommended treatment for depression in children and adolescents may include both individual and family therapy. Cognitive-behavioral therapy and interpersonal psychotherapy have been found to be effective in the treatment of depression. Antidepressant medication may also be helpful, although the Food and Drug Administration (FDA) concluded in 2004 that for some children and adolescents, antidepressants have been found to increase suicidal ideation. Subsequent studies have found a correlation between increased antidepressant prescriptions and lower suicide rates among children and adolescents, but no definitive studies completed to date have substantiated a cause and effect relationship. Caution is needed when prescribing antidepressants to children and adolescents.

TEMPORARY ASSISTANCE TO NEEDY FAMILIES (TANF)

In 1996, the Personal Responsibility and Work Opportunity Reconciliation Act of 1996 was passed, replacing Aid to Families with Dependent Children (AFDC) with Temporary Assistance for Needy Families. This new legislation eliminated cash assistance entitlement programs and transferred responsibility for providing assistance and work opportunities for needy families to the states. The states were given federal funds and wide flexibility to develop and implement their own welfare programs. Citizens apply for assistance at their local TANF agency.

The Office of Family Assistance (OFA) of the United States Department of Health and Human Services, Administration for Children and Families oversees the TANF program. The TANF program was re-authorized in February 2006 under the Deficit Reduction Act of 2005.

Work requirements of TANF:

▶ Recipients (with few exceptions) must work as soon as they are job ready or no later than two years after coming on assistance.

▶ Single parents are required to participate in work activities for at least 30 hours per week. Two-parent families must participate in work activities 35 or 55 hours a week, depending upon circumstances.

▶ Failure to participate in work requirements can result in a reduction or termination of benefits to the family.

▶ States cannot penalize single parents with a child under six for failing to meet work requirements if they cannot find adequate childcare.

▶ States, in fiscal year 2004, had to ensure that 50% of all families and 90% of two-parent families are participating in work activities. If a state reduces its caseload without restricting eligibility, it can receive a caseload reduction credit. This credit reduces the minimum participation rates the state must achieve.

Work activities of TANF:

▶ unsubsidized or TANF subsidized employment
▶ on-the-job training
▶ work experience

- community service
- job search—not to exceed six total weeks and no more than four consecutive weeks
- vocational training—not to exceed 12 months
- job skills training related to work
- satisfactory secondary school attendance
- providing childcare services to individuals who are participating in community service

TANF also has a five-year time limit:

- Families with an adult who has received federally funded assistance for a total of five years (or less at state option) are not eligible for cash aid under the TANF program.
- States may extend assistance beyond 60 months to not more than 20% of their caseload. They may also elect to provide assistance to families beyond 60 months using state-only funds or Social Services Block Grants (U.S. Department of Health and Human Services 2006).

PUBLIC HOUSING AND ASSISTANCE

The rates of homelessness in the United States increased dramatically in the 1980s under President Reagan's administration and continued to spiral through the 1990s and beyond. The increase in homelessness is attributable to a range of factors, including rising housing costs, deinstitutionalization of both mentally disabled persons and persons with development disabilities, cuts in funding for community support programs, and the return of Vietnam veterans.

The passage of the Steward B. McKinney Homeless Assistance Act of 1987 heralded the beginning of grant-in-aid structures and other housing assistance programs to emerge. These programs provided emergency shelters, transitional housing, outreach, and case management services primarily to homeless mentally disabled persons. Although these programs began to ease the burden of homelessness for some groups, they did not go far enough; homelessness continued to flourish, affecting disproportionate numbers of people of color, women with children, and those unable to find affordable housing. According to NASW, a number of factors put individuals at risk for homelessness. These factors include, "alcoholism, drug abuse, low education and illiteracy, sexual exploitation, chronic mental disability, developmental disabilities, or mild mental retardation, and HIV/AIDS" (2001, 185).

Housing Assistance Programs for Low-Income Families and the Homeless

Through the United States Department of Housing and Urban Development (HUD), federal subsidies and grants are available to provide housing assistance to low-income, elderly, disabled, and homeless individuals and families. The Housing Choice Vouchers Program provides housing subsidies to low-income families, elderly persons, and individuals with disabilities. Assistance to homeless individuals and families is made available through grant funding to local communities that have developed continuum of care systems. Funding for these programs has been reduced under recent administrations. Currently, there is not enough funding available to meet the housing needs of low-income and homeless individuals and families.

Housing Choice Vouchers Program

The HUD website offers the following information about housing choice vouchers, more commonly known as Section 8 housing:

> The housing choice voucher program is the federal government's major program for assisting very low-income families, the elderly, and the disabled to afford decent, safe, and sanitary housing in the private market. Since housing assistance is provided on behalf of the family or individual, participants are able to find their own housing, including single-family homes, townhouses and apartments. The participant is free to choose any housing that meets the requirements of the program and is not limited to units located in subsidized housing projects.

According to HUD, housing choice vouchers are administered locally by public housing agencies. The public housing agencies receive federal funds from HUD in order to administer the voucher program.

Determining Eligibility

Caseworkers employed by the local public housing agencies have responsibility for:

▶ collecting information on family composition, income, and assets
▶ verifying accuracy of information with other local agencies, employers, and banks
▶ determining eligibility and the amount of the housing assistance voucher
▶ placing the applicant on a waiting list and notifying applicant when his/her name is reached

Local Preferences and Waiting Lists

Often there are long waiting lists for the housing choice voucher program. Preferences may be given to families who are homeless or living in substandard housing; are currently paying more than 50% of their income for rent; or have been involuntarily displaced. Each public housing agency has the discretion to establish local preferences to reflect the housing needs and priorities of its particular community.

The public housing caseworker is responsible for approving the housing unit to ensure that it is safe and habitable, and that the rent is reasonable and within guidelines established for the applicant. Then the caseworkers arrange for the landlord, the family, and the housing agency to enter into a contract that runs for the same terms as the lease, stipulating the responsibilities and obligations of the landlord, the family (tenant), and the housing agency. Other responsibilities of the housing caseworker are to reassess income and eligibility on an annual basis and to ensure that the housing unit meets the minimum quality housing standards.

Homelessness Assistance

A continuum of care system is designed to address the critical problem of homelessness through a coordinated community-based process of identifying needs and building a system to address those needs. The approach is predicated on the understanding that homelessness is not caused merely by a lack of shelter, but involves a variety of underlying, unmet needs—physical, economic, and social.

The Department of Housing and Urban Development offers the following information about housing programs for the homeless on its website:

▶ **Supportive Housing Programs**
Provides housing, including housing units and group quarters, that have a supportive environment and include a planned service component.

▶ **Shelter Plus Care Programs**
Provides grants for rental assistance for homeless persons with disabilities through four component programs: Tenant, Sponsor, Project, and Single Room Occupancy Rental Assistance.

▶ **Single Room Occupancy Programs**
Provides rental assistance on behalf of homeless individuals in connection with moderate rehabilitation of SRO dwellings.

Other Housing Programs

▶ **Title V Program**
HUD collects and publishes information about surplus federal property that can be used to help homeless persons. Eligible grantees include states, local governments, and nonprofit organizations (United States Department of Housing and Urban Development n.d.).

ADDITIONAL RESOURCES ON THE WEB

Public Health

American Public Health Association
http://www.apha.org

Center for Economic and Social Rights—Right to Health
http://www.cesr.org/health

Disabilities

Center for Law and Social Policy
http://www.clasp.org

Disability and Independent Living Movement History
http://bancroft.berkeley.edu/collections/drilm

DRM Web Watcher Guide to Disabilities Resources on the Internet
http://www.disabilityresources.org

Job Accommodation Network
http://www.jan.wvu.edu

The New Freedom Initiative's Online Resource for Americans with Disabilities
http://www.disabilityinfo.gov

World Health Organization
http://www.who.int/en

Aging

Direct Care Alliance
http://www.directcarealliance.org

Family Caregiver Alliance
http://www.caregiver.org

Federal Long-Term Care Insurance Program
http://www.opm.gov/insure/ltc

National Association for Home Care and Hospice
http://www.nahc.org

National Center for Assisted Living
http://www.ncal.org

National Citizens' Coalition for Nursing Home Reform
http://www.nccnhr.org

Social Work with Children

Accreditation Criteria to become Certified Advanced Children, Youth, and Family Social Worker (C-ACYFSW)
http://www.socialworkers.org/credentials/specialty/C-ACYFSW.asp

Child Welfare Information Gateway
http://www.childwelfare.gov

Forum on Child and Family Statistics
http://www.childstats.gov

NASW Standards for Social Work Practice in Child Welfare
http://www.socialworkers.org/practice/standards/NASWChildWelfare
Standards0905.pdf

U.S. Department of Health & Human Services—Administration for Children and Families
http://www.acf.dhhs.gov

Child Abuse

National MCH Center for Child Death Review
http://www.childdeathreview.org

National Center on Child Fatality Review
http://www.ican-ncfr.org

National Citizens Review Panels
http://www.uky.edu/SocialWork/crp

National Fetal and Infant Mortality Review Program
http://www.acog.org/goto/nfimr

Identifying Child Abuse and Neglect
http://www.childwelfare.gov/can/identifying

Preventing Child Abuse and Neglect
http://www.childwelfare.gov/preventing

Public Housing

Center on Housing Rights and Evictions
http://www.cohre.org

U.S. Department of Housing & Urban Development
http://www.hud.gov

National Housing Institute
http://www.nhi.org

National Council of State Housing Agencies
http://www.ncsha.org

Citizens' Housing and Planning Association
http://www.chapa.org

CHAPTER four

EDUCATIONAL PROGRAMS

CASEWORK IS a great profession for those who want to help others achieve a better life. But while wanting to help others is a necessary component of a successful career in casework, it is not sufficient on its own.

JOB OUTLOOK OPPORTUNITIES

The numbers of retiring and aging baby boomers who will soon be in need of services is rising dramatically and, as a result of this and other demographic changes, the continuing need for caseworkers will increase. The

U.S. Department of Labor projects the job growth in social assistance jobs to be as follows:

> Projected job growth is due mostly to the expansion of services for the elderly and the aging baby-boom generation. Similarly, services for the mentally ill, the physically disabled, and families in crisis will be expanded. Increasing emphasis on providing home care services rather than more costly nursing home or hospital care, and on earlier and better integration of the physically disabled and mentally ill into society, also will contribute to employment growth in the social assistance industry, as will increased demand for drug and alcohol abuse prevention programs. Employment in private social service agencies may be spurred as state and local governments contract out their social services in an effort to cut costs. The expansion and creation of employment in the social assistance industry may depend, in large part, on the amount of funding made available by the government and managed-care organizations (U.S. Department of Labor n.d.).

Trained caseworkers will be needed in the areas of helping the homeless; providing services to troubled and emotionally disturbed children and adolescents; training the unemployed or underemployed; assisting individuals and families in obtaining financial assistance, housing, and other entitlement programs; helping families to stay together; arranging foster care services and adoptions; working with older adults; assisting people with mental illnesses; and many other areas of service. In order to qualify for positions in the above areas, you will need to think about pursuing advanced training in social services, human services, or social work.

In this chapter, you will learn how to identify an educational program and institution that will prepare you for the kind of position that you are looking for. You will also find out about different certificates and academic degrees that are available (including associate's, bachelor's, and master's), the course requirements necessary for graduation from each program, and the kinds of jobs and opportunities that will be available to you upon graduation.

CHOOSING THE RIGHT PROGRAM

Choosing the right program will depend upon a number of factors, including how much education you have had up until now, the kind of job and field that you want to go into, the kinds of skills that you are interested in obtaining, the geographical location in which you would like to live while you study, and how much money and time you are willing to invest in your education.

If you are still in high school or have just started an academic program, you may not yet know just what you would like to do following completion of your studies. The following questions may help you identify your specific interests, whether you are just beginning your career or thinking about pursuing academic training.

- ▶ What age group would you most like to work with?
- ▶ What field of practice would you like to work in (disability, housing assistance, child welfare, mental health, aging, or counseling)?
- ▶ What position would you like to ultimately hold (e.g., human services assistant, social services assistant, social worker, clinical social worker)?
- ▶ How much time are you willing or able to devote to your education (total number of months/years)?
- ▶ How much money can you afford to spend for your education? (Remember that financial aid is available for most programs.)
- ▶ What kinds of knowledge or skills do you hope to learn?
- ▶ How flexible is your schedule? Can you attend classes during the day?
- ▶ Do you need to attend only in the evening? Are you interested in taking classes online?
- ▶ Are you willing to travel or relocate?

The Knowledge You Will Gain

Make a list of subjects (courses) you would like to take. For example, would you like to learn about mental health counseling? Are you interested in learning about food stamp programs or childcare services for new parents? Would you like to learn more about childhood development? Are you interested in learning more about how to provide services to the aging?

Then, compare your list of ideal subjects to courses that are offered within existing programs in human services, human development, and social work. For example, in human services programs, typical courses might include Introduction to Counseling, Child Development, and Substance Abuse Treatment. Typical courses within social work programs will often include Human Development in the Social Environment, Casework with Individuals, Families and Groups, Social Policy and Programs, and Multi-Cultural Practice. You will probably derive the greatest enjoyment and satisfaction from a program that focuses on the topics you would most like to learn about in greater depth. You should also read the mission statement that is listed on the program's website. This will give you an idea of the philosophy and goals of the program. You should try to choose the program that best fits your underlying values, beliefs, and learning style.

Jobs Available after Program Completion

Before you choose a particular program of study in human services or social work, you should first find out what kinds of jobs that program will prepare you to obtain. You might want to look at jobs that are currently available in your area of interest, and find out what kinds of qualifications or credentials are necessary. You might also think about speaking to individuals who are currently working in the field, or contact program directors to find out what kinds of qualifications are required for the jobs in which you are interested. Time permitting, program directors and administrators are sometimes able to schedule informational interviews for prospective employees. Another way to find out about job prospects following graduation is to contact the college or university directly and ask if you can speak to someone who might be able to provide you with post-graduate job information.

DEGREE PROGRAMS IN HUMAN SERVICES AND SOCIAL WORK

Most social assistance, human services, and social work jobs require specific kinds of prerequisite experience and education. For example, some social assistance and human service jobs require a combination of related work experience or college courses in human services, social work, or one of the social or behavioral sciences. Other jobs require an associate degree or a bachelor's degree in human services or social work. Some jobs offer inservice training, such as seminars and workshops.

Entry-level jobs for social workers generally require a bachelor's degree in social work or in an undergraduate major such as psychology or sociology. Most agencies that offer clinical services to clients require workers to have a master's degree in social work or a closely related field; increasingly, agencies and private practice clinics that offer clinical or consultative services require an advanced degree and licensure in clinical social work. Programs in human services or social work offer specific courses at each level of academic training and for each degree that is achieved.

For example, an associate's degree in human services or social work typically takes two years to complete and prepares graduates for entry-level careers as social and human services assistants. The associate's degree requires both foundation courses in liberal arts and science and courses specific to human services or social work. Common courses include abnormal psychology, introduction to gerontology, and developmental psychology. An associate's degree typically takes two years to complete and is considered to be excellent preparation for a bachelor's degree program. Courses taken in an associate's degree in social work often can be credited toward a bachelor's in social work (BSW) degree. Associate's degree programs are most commonly found at community and technical colleges.

A bachelor's degree in human services or social work at most schools combines specific career-related courses with broad exposure to arts and humanities. By the end of a bachelor's program, students will have gained the ability to relate to clients on multiple levels. A bachelor's degree often requires classes in abnormal psychology, group dynamics, developmental psychology, ethics and human services, and research design and evaluation.

Social workers are required to have a bachelor's degree in social work or higher; however, in some states, non-BSW holders may have the title of social worker if their undergraduate degree meets state certification requirements and they have had core courses in social work. A bachelor's degree is the minimum education required to become an entry-level social worker. Bachelor's degrees usually take four years to complete and require both general education courses and courses specific to social work. BSW courses often focus on social work values and ethics, working with a diverse population, social welfare policies, and human growth and development. Bachelor's degrees in social work require an internship for graduation.

A master's degree in social work can often provide opportunities for advancement into clinical social work or social services management. Most social workers specialize in an area such as child services, mental health, or school social work. Master's degree programs in social work help to develop these specialties. Supervised fieldwork usually is required. Master's degrees in social work typically take two years to complete and require the completion of a bachelor's degree program before admission. Some master's programs have a one-year advanced standing MSW program for students who already have their BSWs. If you have a BSW, you might want to consider applying to a MSW program that offers an advanced placement option. Many other MSW programs offer part-time options and evening classes. Others offer courses online.

CERTIFICATE PROGRAMS

In addition to degree programs, certificate programs also allow professionals to expand and refine their skills in a specific area of study. These certificate programs vary in terms of their prerequisites; some require only a high school diploma, while others require that professionals have an academic degree. Some may be taken for credit and applied to degree programs. Other certificate programs are noncredit and may be used to obtain Continuing Education Units, or CEUs. A CEU is a nationally recognized unit of measurement for noncredit continuing education programs. They are designed to document learning experiences for employers and professional organizations. Some examples of certificate programs include certificates in substance abuse counseling, child development, child development home visitor, human services, and gerontology.

The NASW Credentialing Center offers specialty certifications for social workers. Specialty certifications for BSW-level workers include Social Worker in Gerontology; Certified Children, Youth, and Family Social Worker; and Certified Social Work Case Manager. Specialty Certification for MSW-level workers include Clinical Social Worker in Gerontology; Certified Advance Children, Youth, and Family Social Worker; Certified Social Worker in Health Care; Certified Clinical Alcohol, Tobacco, and Other Drugs Social Worker; Certified Advanced Social Work Case Manager; and Certified School Social Work Specialist.

CHOOSING THE RIGHT INSTITUTION

Once you have decided what kind of certificate or degree program you would like to pursue, you must then choose which college or institution that you would like to attend. In choosing a prospective program, you might want to consider the following variables:

▶ the academic strength of the program
▶ the location and size of the institution
▶ the cost and flexibility of the program
▶ the admission requirements

Academics

The academic strength of a program is an important consideration when choosing a college or institution. If you are planning on pursuing advanced education in human services or social work, you will want to be sure that the program is accredited by the national accrediting body for that profession. Employers may require that you have graduated from an accredited program. Admission to advanced degree programs in your field of study may also require that your prior degree was from an accredited program. Also, licensing requirements may insist that your professional degree was obtained from an accredited program.

The Council for Standards in Human Service Education (CSHSE), created in 1976, is the sole national accrediting body for academic programs in human services. Similarly, the Council on Social Work Education is the only accrediting body for academic programs in social work. In order for a program to become accredited by its national accrediting body, it must meet minimum standards of excellence.

CSHSE has issued a listing of all currently accredited human services programs. This listing may be obtained at http://www.cshse.org/accredited.html. For accredited social work programs and programs under candidacy for accreditation as of 2006, please see CSWE's directory of accredited programs at http://www.cswe.org/CSWE/accreditation.

You may also wish to find out the program's academic reputation or ranking. Ranking is usually dependent upon a number of factors, including the number of articles that faculty members publish in top academic journals. A renowned program will attract top students and faculty and may offer more research or internship opportunities. However, while highly ranked research universities may place higher value on the faculty's research productivity, other schools, such as community colleges or lesser ranked colleges, may boast teaching excellence. While a higher ranked school may have more resources, it may be more expensive. Ultimately, how much you get out of a program will largely depend upon how much effort you are able and willing to put into it.

Location

The location of the school or institution you consider attending will likely be a factor in determining whether or not you will apply for admission. Are you willing to relocate? How far are you willing to commute? How important is it to you to be close to family and friends?

Other considerations may include whether you want to attend school in an urban, suburban, or rural setting. If relocating is not a problem for you, you may want to consider the kinds of field experiences you may wish to have. For example, if you decide to attend school in a large city, you will likely have opportunities to work with diverse populations and experience social and human service issues that are related to living in densely populated urban settings. If, however, you are interested in rural social work, for example, or providing casework services to individuals and families with fewer environmental resources, such as the elderly who live in remote settings, then you may wish to apply to programs in smaller cities.

Size

The size of the school or program may also be a factor in your decision. A large program may offer more opportunities to learn from a variety of faculty with a wide range of expertise. Also, you may have a larger number of potential friends with whom to socialize, and thus enjoy a more vibrant social life. However, a smaller program may allow for a smaller teacher-student ratio and a greater sense of support among fellow students and faculty.

Tuition, Scholarships, and Loan Forgiveness Programs[1]

Programs and institutions vary greatly in terms of tuition costs, local costs of living, financial assistance and incentives, and work-study opportunities. In general, private colleges and universities will be more expensive than public schools, and out-of-state tuition costs will be higher than the cost of attending a school in your own state. Additionally, programs will vary in terms of the kinds of tuition assistance they may offer to students. For example, some social work programs offer tuition remission and stipends for students whose field placements are in agencies that serve the elderly, or other underrepresented service recipients. These placements are usually competitive, and based upon a combination of financial need and merit.

Scholarship Programs

The Association of Gerontology in Higher Education offers several scholarships to social work students who focus their area of study to older adults or senior citizens.

▶ AARP Andrus Foundation Undergraduate Scholarship Program for the Study of Aging and Finance are $5,000 scholarships for a full year that are awarded to undergraduates whose main focus is gerontology.

---

[1]*Source:* http://www.collegescholarships.org/scholarships/social-worker.htm.

► AARP Andrus Foundation Graduate Scholarships are awarded to both master's and doctoral students. Doctoral students receive $15,000, and master's students receive $7,000. Both are for full-year scholarships.

A number of state and national associations also offer their own scholarship programs to social work students who display outstanding academic achievement. Some of these offer scholarships to specific ethnic and racial backgrounds.

► **The Council on Social Work Education** offers the Carl A. Scott Book Scholarships, which target African Americans, Asian Americans, and other students of color. They are $500 monetary awards.

► **The National Association of Social Workers** awards several scholarships in master's and doctoral degree programs. The Verne LaMarr Lyons Scholarship is awarded to a student in a master's degree program who is committed to working with the African American community. The Consuelo W. Gosnell Memorial Scholarship is for social work students in master's degree programs who have committed to working with the Hispanic and American Indian populations or public and nonprofit sectors.

Check with the financial aid office and the admissions office of the programs you are interested in to find out about available scholarships and other financial assistance.

Student Loan Programs

Many students attending graduate school arrange to take out federally subsidized or unsubsidized Stafford Loans. These loans are guaranteed by the United States government. Repayment is deferred until six months following graduation. Interest on subsidized loans does not begin to accrue until the loan is in repayment status. Interest on unsubsidized loans begins to accrue from the time the loan is initially dispersed, but payment of interest and principal is deferred until six months following graduation from the program. Please see http://www.staffordloan.com for more information on Stafford and other student loan programs.

Loan Forgiveness Programs

Several loan forgiveness programs are available to students who agree to take social work positions in underserved areas across the country and within their home states. NASW has identified two federal loans available to social work graduates:

- ▶ **Perkins Loan Forgiveness Program** (check with the financial aid office of your institution for further information): This loan forgiveness program is for social workers working in public or private nonprofit child or family service agencies providing services to high risk children and families from low-income communities or social workers providing early intervention services to infants and toddlers with disabilities in public or private nonprofit agencies under IDEA (Individuals with Disabilities Education Act).
- ▶ **National Health Service Corp** (for further information, please visit http://nhsc.bhpr.hrsa.gov/join_us/lrp.cfm): This loan forgiveness program is for fully trained health professionals, including clinical social workers, who are dedicated to working with the underserved and have qualifying educational loans. These health professionals are eligible to compete for repayment of those loans if they choose to serve in a community of greatest need. In addition to loan repayment, these clinicians receive a competitive salary, some tax relief benefits, and a chance to have a significant impact on a community.

Please check the NASW website for further information about loan forgiveness programs: http://www.socialworkers.org/advocacy/issues/loanForgiveness.asp.

Distance Learning

Increasingly, many academic programs are expanding their courses by including online classes. Additionally, some programs in human services and social work are entirely offered online. In a distance learning program, a student learns from materials supplied over the Internet or through instructional tapes and notes sent by mail, without having to physically attend classes. Distance learning offers greater flexibility in the sense that a student does not have to commute to class and can view course material at times that may be more convenient. A disadvantage to distance learning is that students don't have the opportunity to interact with other students or their instructors in person.

Universities currently offering human services and social work degrees online include Capella University (http://www.capella.edu), which offers graduate degrees in human services and social work specializations; Walden University (http://www.waldenu.edu), which offers a PhD specialization in clinical social work, a PhD in human services, and an MS in mental health counseling; Bellevue University (http://www.bellevue.edu), which offers a bachelor's degree in social services administration; and the University of Phoenix (http://www.phoenix.edu), which offers both an associate's and a bachelor's degree in human services management.

Tips for Choosing the School That Is Right for You

▶ If possible, talk to current students. Ask them about the curriculum and faculty, and what they like most and least about the program and institution.

▶ Read about the current faculty on the program's website. What are their research interests? What courses do they teach? If possible, schedule a time when you can meet them in person to discuss the program and whether the program might be a good fit for you and your particular interests.

▶ If possible, sit in on a class. Notice the culture of the classroom; how involved are the students in the class discussion and activities? Pay attention to whether you are engaged by the class and whether you would want to be enrolled in the class.

Admission Requirements

Programs will differ in terms of their admissions requirements. Some colleges and institutions require a minimum grade point average (GPA); others require that you have had relevant work or volunteer experience; still others may require that you have completed specific coursework or have obtained prior degrees. For admission to an associate's or bachelor's program, you will generally need to have obtained a high school diploma or general equivalency diploma (GED). Some schools will require that you have achieved a minimum GPA. Still others will ask for the results of standardized achievement tests, such as the SAT or the ACT. Most will ask that you provide letters of recommendation from individuals who can attest to your personal character, academic potential, and work habits.

Graduate colleges or institutions will sometimes require that you sit for the Graduate Record Exam (GRE), Miller Analogies Test (MAT), or another standardized achievement test. Other programs will require that you submit previously submitted or graded written work, or that you complete an essay describing your wish to attend their program. International students at all levels who are not native speakers of English are usually required to take the Test of English as a Foreign Language (TOEFL) exam.

CURRICULUM CONTENT OF HUMAN SERVICES PROGRAMS

The Council for Standards in Human Service Education has established the minimum standards to which educational programs at all nondegree and degree-granting levels must adhere in order to comply with national accreditation standards. These curriculum standards apply to human service programs at the technical, associate's degree, and advanced (bachelor's degrees and higher) levels.

Technical Level: Nondegree Granting Certificates

According to the Council for Standards in Human Service Education (CSHSE), nondegree certificate programs must include the following curricular content:

"1. The specifications for technical level training are designed for a course of study that provides skills, knowledge, and field experience necessary for the beginning level human service worker.

2. Since many technical-level training programs are designed for specific jobs or state registration requirements, the specifications are written to enable programs to meet these requirements while also meeting the needs of students who want to continue their education. The technical level specifications permit training that emphasizes either a moderately broad range of generic competencies or a concentration in a specialized area.

3. Planning and evaluation skill development shall concentrate on competencies needed in relation to specific client goals.

4. Information gathering skill development shall emphasize observation and interviewing techniques.

5. Intervention skills shall be developed to a level appropriate for use under direct supervision and include either a concentration in specialized competencies or a broader range of generic competencies, depending on the program objectives.

6. Fieldwork: 180 hours."

Associate's Degree in Human Services

According to CSHSE, associate's degree programs must include the following curricular content:

"1. The historical and social contexts of human services; models of human development and group dynamics; models for individual and small group change; and the characteristics of client populations with special human service needs.

2. Planning and evaluation skills that focus on the attainment of basic case managing skills, the analysis of the needs of clients, and design and implementation of a simple plan of action.

3. Information management skills that center on obtaining and using client data, record keeping and report writing, interpersonal communication, and active listening.

4. Intervention skills and strategies that are centered on provision of direct services to individuals and groups and the major related roles such as advocate, broker, evaluator, teacher, and caregiver.

5. Fieldwork: 250 hours."

Graduate-Level Degree

CSHSE requires that graduate-level programs must include the following curricular content:

"1. The specifications for the Advanced (Bachelor or Master) Degree Level include those from the Technical and Associate Degree Levels, and increase the student's knowledge of how cultural variations and regional differences define standards and needs.
2. The curriculum includes the study of more complex human systems, as well as advocacy, and change within those systems.
3. Program planning, design, and evaluation knowledge and skills are included in the curriculum.
4. Information management includes the knowledge and skills to conduct needs assessment studies and community education programs.
5. Intervention skills shall include increased attention to broadening the scope, variety, and mastery of helping and change modalities and are expanded to include interventions focused on problems inherent to the service delivery or other larger systems.
6. Administration and supervision skills appropriate for directing small programs or units of larger programs are included in the curriculum.
7. Fieldwork: 350 hours."

SOCIAL WORK PROGRAMS

The Council on Social Work Education offers the following statement about social work education:

Social work education is grounded in the liberal arts and contains a coherent, integrated professional foundation in social work. The graduate advanced curriculum is built from the professional foundation. Graduates of baccalaureate and master's social work programs demonstrate the capacity to meet the foundation objectives and objectives unique to the program. Graduates of master's social work programs also demonstrate the capacity to meet advanced program objectives (CSWE 2001).

Bachelor's and Master's Level Social Work Education: Foundation Curriculum Content

According to CSWE, both BSW- and MSW-level social work programs must provide foundation curriculum content in the following areas:

Values and Ethics

Social work education programs integrate content about values and principles of ethical decision making as presented in the National Association of Social Workers Code of Ethics. The educational experience provides students with the opportunity to be aware of personal values; develop, demonstrate, and promote the values of the profession; and analyze ethical dilemmas and the ways in which these affect practice, services, and clients.

Diversity

Social work programs integrate content that promotes understanding, affirmation, and respect for people from diverse backgrounds. The content emphasizes the interlocking and complex nature of culture and personal identity. It ensures that social services meet the needs of groups served and are culturally relevant. Programs educate students to recognize diversity within and between groups that may influence assessment, planning, intervention, and research. Students learn how to define, design, and implement strategies for effective practice with persons from diverse backgrounds.

Populations-at-Risk and Social and Economic Justice

Social work education programs integrate content on populations-at-risk, examining the factors that contribute to and constitute being at risk. Programs educate students to identify how group membership influences access to resources, and present content on the dynamics of such risk factors and responsive and productive strategies to redress them. Programs integrate social and economic justice content grounded in an understanding of distributive justice, human and civil rights, and the global interconnections of oppression. Programs provide content related to implementing strategies to combat discrimination, oppression, and economic deprivation and to promote social and economic justice. Programs prepare students to advocate for nondiscriminatory social and economic systems.

Human Behavior and the Social Environment
Social work education programs provide content on the reciprocal relationships between human behavior and social environments. Content includes empirically based theories and knowledge that focus on the interactions between and among individuals, groups, societies, and economic systems. It includes theories and knowledge of biological, sociological, cultural, psychological, and spiritual development across the life span; the range of social systems in which people live (individual, family, group, organizational, and community); and the ways social systems promote or deter people in maintaining or achieving health and well-being.

Social Welfare Policy and Services
Programs provide content about the history of social work, the history and current structures of social welfare services, and the role of policy in service delivery, social work practice, and attainment of individual and social well-being. Course content provides students with knowledge and skills to understand major policies that form the foundation of social welfare; analyze organizational, local, state, national, and international issues in social welfare policy and social service delivery; analyze and apply the results of policy research relevant to social service delivery; understand and demonstrate policy practice skills in regard to economic, political, and organizational systems, and use them to influence, formulate, and advocate for policy consistent with social work values; and identify financial, organizational, administrative, and planning processes required to deliver social services.

Social Work Practice

Social work practice content is anchored in the purposes of the social work profession and focuses on strengths, capacities, and resources of client systems in relation to their broader environments. Students learn practice content that encompasses knowledge and skills to work with individuals, families, groups, organizations, and communities. This content includes engaging clients in an appropriate working relationship, identifying issues, problems, needs, resources, and assets; collecting and assessing information; and planning for service delivery. It includes using communication skills, supervision, and consultation. Practice content also includes identifying, analyzing, and implementing empirically based interventions designed to achieve client goals; applying empirical knowledge and technological advances; evaluating program outcomes and practice effectiveness; developing, analyzing, advocating, and providing leadership for policies and services; and promoting social and economic justice.

Research

Qualitative and quantitative research content provides understanding of a scientific, analytic, and ethical approach to building knowledge for practice. The content prepares students to develop, use, and effectively communicate empirically based knowledge, including evidence-based interventions. Research knowledge is used by students to provide high-quality services; to initiate change; to improve practice, policy, and social service delivery; and to evaluate their own practice.

Field Education

Field education is an integral component of social work education anchored in the mission, goals, and educational level of the program. It occurs in settings that reinforce students' identification with the purposes, values, and ethics of the profession; fosters the integration of empirical and practice-based knowledge;

and promotes the development of professional competence. Field education is systematically designed, supervised, coordinated, and evaluated on the basis of criteria by which students demonstrate the achievement of program objectives.

Master's Level Social Work Education (Advanced Curriculum Content)

The master's curriculum prepares graduates for advanced social work practice in an area of concentration. Using a conceptual framework to identify advanced knowledge and skills, programs build an advanced curriculum from the foundation content. In the advanced curriculum, the foundation content areas are addressed in greater depth, breadth, and specificity and support the program's conception of advanced practice (CSWE 2001).

LICENSING

Licensing requirements of human service workers and social workers vary across the country; some states require that workers be licensed in order to provide casework services to clients and others do not. More recently, efforts have been under way to require individuals who provide casework services to vulnerable populations and groups be licensed by the state in which services are provided. However, in many states caseworkers are not required to be licensed at all. For example, child protective workers are often not licensed. Given the recent spiral in high profile cases of child abuse and child fatalities, there is increasing pressure to ensure that workers who are investigating cases of child abuse are properly licensed.

The following table provided by the Association of Social Work Boards (ASWB) website illustrates various levels of social work practice and how they are regulated according to the state in which the services are provided. (Please be advised that these regulations are subject to change. Check with the individual state for any updated information.)

Title	Initials	Education	Experience	Exam Required	Board Approval
Alabama					
Private Independent Practice (Certif.)	PIP	DSW/MSW	2 years post	N/R	Not applicable
Licensed Certified Social Worker	LCSW	DSW/MSW	2 years post	Clinical/ Advanced Generalist	Yes
Licensed Graduate Social Worker	LGSW	DSW/MSW	0	Master's	Yes
Licensed Bachelor Social Worker	LBSW	BSW	0	Bachelor's	Yes
Alaska					
Licensed Clinical Social Worker	LCSW	DSW/MSW	2 years post	Clinical	Yes
Licensed Master Social Worker	LMSW	DSW/MSW	0	Master's	Yes
Licensed Baccalaureate Social Worker	LBSW	BSW	0	Bachelor's	Yes
Alberta					
Registered Social Worker—Clinical	RSW	DSW/MSW	2 years post	Clinical	Yes
Registered Social Worker	RSW	SW degree or diploma	1,500 hours	N/R	Not applicable
Arizona					
Licensed Clinical Social Worker	LCSW	DSW/MSW	2 years post	Clinical	Yes
Licensed Master Social Worker	LMSW	DSW/MSW	0	Master's	Yes
Licensed Bachelor Social Worker	LBSW	BSW	0	Bachelor's	Yes
Arkansas					
Licensed Certified Social Worker	LCSW	MSW	2 years post	Clinical/ Advanced Generalist	Yes
Licensed Master Social Worker	LMSW	MSW	0	Master's	Yes
Licensed Social Worker	LSW	BSW	0	Bachelor's	Yes

Title	Initials	Education	Experience	Exam Required	Board Approval
British Columbia					
Registered Social Worker	RSW	BSW/MSW	0	N/R	Yes
Registered Social Worker—Private Practice	RSW-P	DSW/MSW	2 years post	N/R	Yes
Registered Social Worker—Clinical	RSW	MSW	3,000 hours post	Clinical	Yes
California					
Licensed Clinical Social Worker	LCSW	MSW	2 years post	N/R	Not applicable
Associate Clinical Social Worker	ASW	MSW	0	N/R	Not applicable
Colorado					
Licensed Clinical Social Worker	LCSW	DSW/MSW	1 year/ 2 years post	Clinical/ Advanced Generalist	Yes
Licensed Social Worker	LSW	MSW	0	Master's/ Advanced Generalist/ Clinical	Yes
Connecticut					
Licensed Clinical Social Worker	LCSW	DSW/MSW	3,000 hours post	Clinical	Yes
Delaware					
Licensed Clinical Social Worker	LCSW	DSW/MSW	2 years post	Clinical	Yes
District of Columbia					
Licensed Independent Clinical Social Worker	LICSW	DSW/MSW	3,000 hours post	Clinical	Yes
Licensed Independent Social Worker	LISW	DSW/MSW	3,000 hours post	Advanced Generalist	Yes
Licensed Graduate Social Worker	LGSW	DSW/MSW	0	Master's	Yes
Licensed Social Work Associate	LSWA	BSW	0	Bachelor's	Yes

(continued)

Title	Initials	Education	Experience	Exam Required	Board Approval
Florida					
Licensed Clinical Social Worker	LCSW	DSW/MSW	2 years post	Clinical	Yes
Certified Master Social Worker	CMSW	MSW	2 years post	Master's	Yes
Georgia					
Licensed Clinical Social Worker	LCSW	MSW	3 years post	Clinical/ Advanced Generalist	Yes
Licensed Master Social Worker	LMSW	MSW	0	Master's	Yes
Hawaii					
Licensed Clinical Social Worker	LCSW	DSW/MSW	3,000 hours post	Clinical	Yes
Licensed Social Worker	LSW	DSW/MSW	0	Master's	Yes
Licensed Bachelor Social Worker	LBSW	BSW	0	Bachelor's	Yes
Idaho					
Licensed Clinical Social Worker	LCSW	DSW/MSW	2 years post	Clinical	Yes
Licensed Master Social Worker— Independent	LMSWI	MSW	2 years post	Master's	Yes
Licensed Master Social Worker	LMSW	DSW/MSW	0	Master's	Yes
Licensed Social Worker—Independent	LSWI	BSW	2 years post	Bachelor's	Yes
Licensed Social Worker	LSW	BSW	0	Bachelor's	Yes
Illinois					
Licensed Clinical Social Worker	LCSW	DSW	2,000 hours post	Clinical	No
Licensed Clinical Social Worker	LCSW	MSW	3,000 hours post	Clinical	No
Licensed Social Worker	LSW	MSW	0	Master's	No
Licensed Social Worker	LSW	BSW	3 years post	Master's	No

Title	Initials	Education	Experience	Exam Required	Board Approval
Indiana					
Licensed Clinical Social Worker	LCSW	DSW/MSW	2 years post	Clinical	Yes
Licensed Social Worker	LSW	BSW	2 years post	Master's	Yes
Licensed Social Worker	LSW	MSW	0	Master's	Yes
Iowa					
Licensed Independent Social Worker	LISW	DSW/MSW	2 years post	Clinical	Yes
Licensed Master Social Worker	LMSW	DSW/MSW	0	Master's	Yes
Licensed Bachelor Social Worker	LBSW	BSW	0	Bachelor's	Yes
Kansas					
Licensed Specialist Clinical Social Worker	LSCSW	DSW/MSW	2 years post	Clinical	Yes
Licensed Master Social Worker	LMSW	MSW	0	Master's	Yes
Licensed Bachelor Social Worker	LBSW	BSW	0	Bachelor's	Yes
Kentucky					
Licensed Clinical Social Worker	LCSW	DSW/MSW	2 years post	Clinical	Yes
Certified Social Worker	CSW	DSW/MSW	0	Master's	Yes
Licensed Social Worker	LSW	BSW	0	Bachelor's	Yes
Licensed Social Worker	LSW	BA	2 years post	Bachelor's	Yes
Louisiana					
Licensed Clinical Social Worker	LCSW	MSW	3 years post	Clinical/ Advanced Generalist	Yes
Graduate Social Worker	GSW	MSW	0	Master's	Yes
Registered Social Worker	RSW	BSW/BA/BS	0	N/R	Yes

(continued)

Title	Initials	Education	Experience	Exam Required	Board Approval
Maine					
Licensed Clinical Social Worker	LCSW	DSW/MSW	2 years post	Clinical	Yes
Certified Social Worker—Independent Practice	CSW-IP	DSW/MSW	2 years post	Clinical	Yes
Licensed Master Social Worker	LMSW	DSW/MSW	0	Master's	Yes
Licensed Master Social Worker— Clinical Conditional	LMSW-CC	DSW/MSW	2 years post	Master's	Yes
Licensed Social Worker	LSW	BSW	0	Bachelor's	Yes
Licensed Social Worker	LSW	BA/BS in related field	3,200 hours	Bachelor's	Yes
Licensed Social Worker—Conditional	LSW-C	BA/BS in related field	2 years post	N/R	Yes
Manitoba					
Registered Social Worker	RSW	BSW/MSW	0	N/R	Not applicable
Maryland					
Licensed Certified Social Worker— Clinical	LCSW-C	MSW	2 years post	Clinical	Yes
Licensed Certified Social Worker	LCSW	MSW	2 years post LGSW	Advanced Generalist	Yes
Licensed Graduate Social Worker	LGSW	MSW	0	Master's	Yes
Licensed Social Work Associate	LSWA	BSW	0	Bachelor's	Yes
Massachusetts					
Licensed Independent Clinical Social Worker	LICSW	DSW/MSW	2 years post	Clinical	Yes
Licensed Certified Social Worker	LCSW	DSW/MSW	0	Master's	Yes
Licensed Social Worker	LSW	BSW	0	Bachelor's	Yes
Licensed Social Worker	LSW	BA/BS	2 years	Bachelor's	Yes

Title	Initials	Education	Experience	Exam Required	Board Approval
Licensed Social Worker	LSW	HS Diploma	10 years	Bachelor's	Yes
Licensed Social Worker	LSW	1 year college	8 years	Bachelor's	Yes
Licensed Social Worker	LSW	2 years college	6 years	Bachelor's	Yes
Licensed Social Worker	LSW	2.5 years college	5 years	Bachelor's	Yes
Licensed Social Work Associate	LSWA	HS Diploma	4 years post	Associate	Yes
Licensed Social Work Associate	LSWA	AA	0	Associate	Yes
Licensed Social Work Associate	LSWA	BA/BS	0	Associate	Yes
Michigan					
Licensed Master Social Worker—Clinical	LMSW-C	MSW	2 years post	Clinical	Yes
Licensed Master Social Worker—Macro	LMSW-M	MSW	2 years post	Advanced Generalist	Yes
Licensed Bachelor Social Worker	LBSW	BSW	2 years post	Bachelor's	Yes
Social Service Technician	SWT	Associate's degree in SW	350 hours	N/R	Yes
Social Service Technician	SWT	2 years college with 4 courses in human services	0	N/R	Yes
Social Service Technician	SWT	HS Diploma	2,000 hours over at least one year	N/R	Yes
Minnesota					
Licensed Independent Clinical Social Worker	LICSW	DSW/MSW	2 years post	Clinical	Yes
Licensed Independent Social Worker	LISW	DSW/MSW	2 years post	Advanced Generalist	Yes

(continued)

Title	Initials	Education	Experience	Exam Required	Board Approval
Licensed Graduate Social Worker	LGSW	DSW/MSW	0	Master's	Yes
Licensed Social Worker	LSW	BSW	0	Bachelor's	Yes
Mississippi					
Licensed Certified Social Worker	LCSW	DSW/MSW	2 years post	Clinical/ Advanced Generalist	Yes
Licensed Master Social Worker	LMSW	DSW/MSW	0	Master's	Yes
Licensed Social Worker	LSW	BSW	0	Bachelor's	Yes
Missouri					
Licensed Clinical Social Worker	LCSW	DSW/MSW	2 years post	Clinical	Yes
Provisional Licensed Clinical Social Worker	PLCSW	DSW/MSW	0	Clinical	Yes
Licensed Baccalaureate Social Worker	LBSW	BSW	3,000 hours post	Bachelor's	Yes
Provisional Baccalaureate Social Worker	PBLSW	BSW	0	Bachelor's	Yes
Montana					
Licensed Clinical Social Worker	LCSW	DSW/MSW	2 years post	Clinical/ Advanced Generalist	Yes
Nebraska					
Licensed Mental Health Practitioner	LMHP	DSW/MSW	3,000 hours post	Clinical	Yes
Certified Master Social Worker	CMSW	DSW/MSW	3,000 hours post	Clinical/ Advanced Generalist	Yes
Certified Social Worker	CSW	BSW/MSW	0	N/R	Yes
Nevada					
Licensed Clinical Social Worker	LCSW	DSW/MSW	3,000 hours post	Clinical	Yes
Licensed Independent Social Worker	LISW	DSW/MSW	3,000 hours post	Advanced Generalist	Yes
Licensed Social Worker	LSW	BSW/MSW	0	Bachelor's/ Master's	Yes

Title	Initials	Education	Experience	Exam Required	Board Approval
New Brunswick					
Registered Social Worker	RSW	BSW/MSW	0	N/R	Not applicable
New Hampshire					
Licensed Independent Clinical Social Worker	LICSW	DSW/MSW	2 years post	Clinical	Yes
New Jersey					
Licensed Clinical Social Worker	LCSW	DSW/MSW	2 years post	Clinical	No
Licensed Social Worker	LSW	DSW/MSW	0	Master's	No
Certified Social Worker	CSW	BSW	0	N/R	No
Certified Social Worker	CSW	BA/BS in related field	1,600 hours over 18 months, prior to 1995 ONLY	N/R	No
New Mexico					
Licensed Independent Social Worker	LISW	MSW	2 years post	Clinical/ Advanced Generalist	Yes
Licensed Master Social Worker	LMSW	MSW	0	Master's	Yes
Licensed Baccalaureate Social Worker	LBSW	BSW	0	Bachelor's	Yes
New York					
Licensed Clinical Social Worker	LCSW	MSW	3 years post	Clinical	Yes
Licensed Master Social Worker	LMSW	MSW	0	Master's	Yes
Newfoundland & Labrador					
Registered Social Worker	RSW	DSW/MSW/ BSW	0	N/R	Not applicable
North Carolina					
Licensed Clinical Social Worker	LCSW	DSW/MSW	2 years post	Clinical	Yes
Certified Master Social Worker	CMSW	DSW/MSW	0	Master's	Yes
Certified Social Worker	CSW	BSW	0	Bachelor's	Yes

(continued)

Title	Initials	Education	Experience	Exam Required	Board Approval
Certified Social Work Manager	CSWM	DSW/MSW/ BSW	2 years post	Advanced Generalist	Yes
North Dakota					
Licensed Independent Clinical Social Worker	LICSW	DSW/MSW	4 years post	Clinical	Yes
Licensed Certified Social Worker	LCSW	DSW/MSW	0	Master's/ Advanced Generalist/ Clinical	Yes
Licensed Social Worker	LSW	BSW	0	Bachelor's	Yes
Nova Scotia					
Registered Social Worker	RSW	DSW/MSW/ BSW	3 years post	N/R	Not applicable
Registered Social Worker Candidate	RSW-C	DSW/MSW/ BSW	0	N/R	Not applicable
Registered Social Worker—Private Practice	RSW-P	DSW/MSW	4 years post	N/R	Not applicable
Ohio					
Licensed Independent Social Worker	LISW	DSW/MSW	2 years post	Clinical/ Advanced Generalist	Yes
Licensed Social Worker	LSW	DSW/MSW/ BSW	0	Bachelor's	Yes
Registered Social Work Assistant	SWA	AAS	0	N/R	Yes
Oklahoma					
Licensed Clinical Social Worker	LCSW	MSW	2 years post	Clinical	Yes
Licensed Social Worker—Administration	LSW	MSW	2 years post	Advanced Generalist	Yes
Licensed Social Worker	LSW	MSW	2 years post	Advanced Generalist	Yes
Licensed Master Social Worker	LMSW	MSW	0	Master's	Yes
Licensed Social Work Associate	LSWA	BSW	2 years post	Bachelor's	Yes

Title	Initials	Education	Experience	Exam Required	Board Approval
Ontario					
Registered Social Worker	RSW	DSW/MSW/ BSW	0	N/R	Not applicable
Oregon					
Licensed Clinical Social Worker	LCSW	DSW/MSW	2 years post	Clinical	Yes
Clinical Social Work Associate	CSWA	DSW/MSW	0	N/R	Yes
Pennsylvania					
Licensed Clinical Social Worker	LCSW	MSW	3 years post or 3,600 hours	Clinical	Yes
Licensed Social Worker	LSW	MSW	0	Master's	Yes
Provisional Social Worker	PSW	BSW	0	Bachelor's	Yes
Prince Edward Island					
Registered Social Worker	RSW	BSW	0	N/R	Not applicable
Puerto Rico					
Licensed Social Worker	LSW	DSW/MSW	2 years post	N/R	Not applicable
Quebec					
Social Worker	SW	BSW/MSW	0	N/R	Not applicable
Rhode Island					
Licensed Independent Clinical Social Worker	LICSW	DSW/MSW	2 years post	Clinical	Yes
Licensed Clinical Social Worker	LCSW	MSW	0	Master's	Yes
Saskatchewan					
Registered Social Worker	RSW	Certificate in social work	0	N/R	Not applicable
South Carolina					
Licensed Independent Social Worker—AP	LISW-AP	DSW/MSW	2 years post	Advanced Generalist	Yes
Licensed Independent Social Worker—CP	LISW-CP	DSW/MSW	2 years post	Clinical	Yes

(continued)

Title	Initials	Education	Experience	Exam Required	Board Approval
Licensed Master Social Worker	LMSW	DSW/MSW	0	Master's	Yes
Licensed Baccalaureate Social Worker	LBSW	BSW	0	Bachelor's	Yes
South Dakota					
Private Independent Practice	CSW-PIP	DSW/MSW	2 years post	Clinical/ Advanced Generalist	Yes
Certified Social Worker	CSW	DSW/MSW	0	Master's	Yes
Social Worker	SW	BSW	0	Bachelor's	Yes
Social Worker	SW	BA	2 years post	Bachelor's	Yes
Social Work Associate	SWA	AA/BA	0	Associate	Yes
Tennessee					
Licensed Clinical Social Worker—Independent Practitioner	LCSW	DSW/MSW	2 years post	Clinical	Yes
Certified Master Social Worker	CMSW	DSW/MSW	0	N/R	Yes
Licensed Clinical Social Worker—Reciprocity	LCSW	DSW/MSW	2 years post	Clinical	Yes
Texas					
Licensed Clinical Social Worker	LCSW	DSW/MSW	3,000 hours post	Clinical	Yes
Licensed Master Social Worker—Advanced Practice	LMSW-AP	DSW/MSW	3,000 hours post	Advanced Generalist	Yes
Licensed Master Social Worker	LMSW	DSW/MSW	0	Master's	Yes
Licensed Baccalaureate Social Worker	LBSW	BSW	0	Bachelor's	Yes
Utah					
Licensed Clinical Social Worker	LCSW	DSW/MSW	2 years post	Clinical	No
Certified Social Worker	CSW	DSW/MSW	0	Master's	No
Social Service Worker	SSW	BA	1 year	Bachelor's	No
Social Service Worker	SSW	BSW/MSW	0	Bachelor's	No

Title	Initials	Education	Experience	Exam Required	Board Approval
Vermont					
Licensed Clinical Social Worker	LCSW	DSW/MSW	2 years post	Clinical	No
Virgin Islands					
Certified Independent Social Worker	CISW	DSW/MSW	2 years post	Clinical/ Advanced Generalist	Yes
Certified Social Worker	CSW	DSW/MSW	0	Master's	Yes
Social Worker	SW	BSW	0	Bachelor's	Yes
Social Worker	SW	BA	2 years post	Bachelor's	Yes
Social Work Associate	SWA	AA/BA	0	Bachelor's	Yes
Virginia					
Licensed Clinical Social Worker	LCSW	MSW	2 years post	Clinical	Yes
Licensed Social Worker	LSW	MSW	0	Bachelor's	Yes
Licensed Social Worker	LSW	BSW	2 years post	Bachelor's	Yes
Washington					
Licensed Independent Clinical Social Worker	LICSW	DSW/MSW	3 years post	Clinical	Yes
Licensed Advanced Social Worker	LASW	DSW/MSW	2 years post	Advanced Generalist	Yes
West Virginia					
Licensed Independent Clinical Social Worker	LICSW	DSW/MSW	2 years post	Clinical	Yes
Licensed Certified Social Worker	LCSW	DSW/MSW	2 years post	Advanced Generalist	Yes
Licensed Graduate Social Worker	LGSW	MSW	0	Master's	Yes
Licensed Social Worker	LSW	BSW	0	Bachelor's	Yes
Wisconsin					
Licensed Clinical Social Worker	LCSW	DSW/MSW	2 years post	Clinical	Yes
Certified Independent Social Worker	CISW	DSW/MSW	2 years post	Advanced Generalist	Yes

(continued)

Title	Initials	Education	Experience	Exam Required	Board Approval
Certified Advanced Practice Social Worker	CAPSW	DSW/MSW	0	Master's	Yes
Certified Social Worker	CSW	BSW/MSW	0	Bachelor's	Yes
Wyoming					
Licensed Clinical Social Worker	LCSW	DSW/MSW	2 years post	Clinical/ Advanced Generalist	Yes
Provisional Clinical Social Worker	PCSW	DSW/MSW	2 years post	N/R	Not applicable
Certified Social Worker	CSW	BSW	0	Bachelor's/ Master's	Yes

Source: The Association of Social Work Boards, n.d.

Appendix A

List of Professional Organizations

American Public Health Association (APHA)
http://www.apha.org
800 I Street, N.W.
Washington, D.C. 20001
Phone: 202-777-APHA
Fax: 202-777-2533

APHA is an association of individuals and organizations working to improve the public's health and to achieve equity in health status for all. It promotes the scientific and professional foundation of public health practices and policy, advocates the conditions for a healthy global society, emphasizes prevention, and enhances the ability of members to promote and protect environmental and community health.

American Public Human Services Association (APHSA)

http://www.aphsa.org/Home/home_news.asp
810 First Street, N.E., Suite 500
Washington, D.C. 20002
Phone: 202-682-0100
Fax: 202-289-6555

APHSA provides information on available occupations in human services, publications, conferences, policies and issues, leadership and practice, partnership initiatives, and affiliate organizations for those interested in the field of human services. Their mission is to develop and promote policies and practices that improve the health and well-being of families, children, and adults.

Association for Community Organization & Social Administration (ACOSA)

http://www.acosa.org/
20560 Bensley Ave.
Lynwood, IL 60411
Phone: 708-757-4187
Fax: 708-757-4234

ACOSA is a membership organization for community organizers, activists, nonprofit administrators, community builders, policy practitioners, students, and educators with a goal in strengthening community organization and social administration.

Association for Gerontology Education in Social Work (AGESW)

http://www.agesw.org
President Sherry Cummings, PhD
The University of Tennessee
College of Social Work
193 Polk Ave., Suite E
Nashville, TN 37210

The Association for Gerontology Education in Social Work provides leadership and assistance to social work educational programs and professionals in order to advocate for the integration of gerontological content in undergraduate and graduate social work education; to promote the teaching of gerontology to all social workers; and to develop short- and long-term perspectives in relevant curricular developments.

Child Welfare League of America (CWLA)

http://www.cwla.org
Mid-Atlantic Region Office
c/o Board of Child Care
3300 Gaither Road
Baltimore, MD 21244
Phone: 410-496-5607
Fax: 410-496-5624

CWLA is an association of nearly 800 public and private nonprofit agencies that assist more than 3.5 million abused and neglected children and their families each year with a range of services.

Council for Standards in Human Services Education

http://www.cshse.org
c/o Harrisburg Area Community College
Human Services Program
One HACC Dr.
Harrisburg, PA 17110

Council on Social Work Education (CSWE)

http://www.cswe.org
1725 Duke St., Suite 500
Alexandria, VA 22314
Phone: 703-683-8080
Fax: 703-683-8099

CSWE provides information on membership, accreditation, scholarships and fellowships, meetings and education, career and professional services, research and resources, publications, and centers and institutes for the social work student. Their goal is to strengthen the profession of social work through leadership in research, career advancement, and education.

Human Services Administration Organization

http://www.hsao.info
2801 Custer Ave., Suite 1
Pittsburgh, PA 15227
Phone: 412-884-4500
Fax: 412-885-3900

Human Services Administration Organization (HSAO) provides individualized, specialized, and enhanced case management services to both children and adults with behavioral health needs. Their mission is to empower individuals, families, and communities by improving their quality of life through specialized, personalized, enhanced and effective case management.

The International Federation of Social Workers

http://www.ifsw.org/home
P.O. Box 6875
Schwarztorstrasse 22
CH-3001
Berne, Switzerland
Phone: (41) 31 382 6015
Fax: (41) 31 382 1125

The International Federation of Social Workers (IFSW) is a global organization striving for social justice, human rights, and social development through the development of social work, best practices, and international cooperation between social workers and their professional organizations.

National Association of Social Workers (NASW)

http://www.socialworkers.org
750 First St., N.E., Suite 700
Washington, D.C. 20002
Phone: 202-408-8600

The National Association of Social Workers (NASW) is the largest membership organization of professional social workers in the world, with 150,000 members. NASW works to enhance the professional growth and development of its members, to create and maintain professional standards, and to advance sound social policies.

National Human Services Assembly

http://www.nassembly.org
1319 F Street, N.W., Suite 402
Washington, D.C. 20004
Phone: 202-347-2080
Fax: 202-393-4517

The National Human Services Assembly is an association of the nation's leading national nonprofits in the fields of health, human and community development, and human services. The National Assembly is a learning community where leaders with parallel responsibilities at different national nonprofit human service organizations share knowledge and expertise about their work in this sector. It is also a vehicle for collaborative action among its members and other interested parties in the public, private, and nonprofit sectors.

The National Institute of Mental Health (NIMH)

http://www.nimh.nih.gov
6001 Executive Blvd., Room 8184, MSC 9663
Bethesda, MD 20892
Phone: 866-615-6464

The National Institute of Mental Health (NIMH) is the largest scientific organization in the world dedicated to research focused on the understanding, treatment, and prevention of mental disorders and the promotion of mental health.

National Organization for Human Services (NOHS)

http://www.nationalhumanservices.org
90 Madison St., Suite 206
Denver, CO 80206
Phone: 303-320-5430

The vision of the National Organization for Human Services is to strengthen recognition of the unique and valued role of human services professionals.

Society for Social Work and Research (SSWR)

http://www.sswr.org
11240 Waples Mill Rd., Suite 200
Fairfax, VA 22030
Phone: 703-352-7797
Fax: 703-359-7562

The Society for Social Work and Research was founded in 1994 as a free-standing organization dedicated to the advancement of social work research. SSWR works collaboratively with a number of other organizations that are committed to improving support for research among social workers. Members include faculty in schools of social work and other professional schools, research staff in public and private agencies, and master's/doctoral students.

Appendix B

Resources

Children's Defense Fund

http://www.childrensdefense.org
25 E Street, N.W.
Washington, D.C. 20001
Phone: 800-233-1200

The Children's Defense Fund grew out of the civil rights movement under the leadership of Marian Wright Edelman. It has become the nation's strongest voice for children and families since its founding in 1973. CDF traces its heritage to Dr. Martin Luther King, Jr., his Poor People's Campaign, and the Washington Research Project, a nonprofit organization that monitored federal programs for low-income families.

Child Welfare Information Gateway

http://www.childwelfare.gov
c/o Children's Bureau/ACYF
1250 Maryland Avenue, S.W., Eighth Floor
Washington, D.C. 20024
Phone: 800-394-3366

Formerly the National Clearinghouse on Child Abuse and Neglect Information and the National Adoption Information Clearinghouse, Child Welfare Information Gateway provides access to information and resources to help protect children and strengthen families. A service of the Children's Bureau, Administration for Children and Families, U.S. Department of Health and Human Services.

U.S. Department of Health and Human Services

http://www.hhs.gov
200 Independence Ave., S.W.
Washington, D.C. 20201
Phone: 877-696-6775

The Department of Health and Human Services is the United States government's principal agency for protecting the health of all Americans and providing essential human services, especially for those who are least able to help themselves. The Department includes over 300 programs, covering a wide spectrum of activities, including health and social science research, preventing disease, Medicaid and Medicare, and assuring food and drug safety.

National Clearinghouse for Alcohol and Drug Information (NCADI)

http://ncadi.samhsa.gov
11426-28 Rockville Pike
Rockville, MD 20852
Phone: 800-487-4889

The National Clearinghouse for Alcohol and Drug Information is a resource for publications and other materials concerning alcohol and substance abuse prevention, intervention, and treatment. Publication topics include the relationship between substance abuse and child and spouse abuse, fetal alcohol syndrome, fetal alcohol effects, and alternatives in treatment. The Clearinghouse is funded by the Center for Substance Abuse Prevention of the Substance Abuse and Mental Health Services Administration.

National Mental Health Association (NMHA)

http://www.nmha.org
2001 North Beauregard St., 12th Floor
Alexandria, VA 22311
Phone: 703-684-7722

The National Mental Health Association is dedicated to promoting mental health, preventing mental disorders, and achieving victory over mental illnesses through advocacy, education, research, and service. The Association's National Mental Health Information Center (MHIC) offers referrals to mental health services and provides educational material about mental illness and mental health to the public, local mental health associations, corporations, and other mental health organizations.

Office of Minority Health Resource Center (OMH-RC)

http://www.omhrc.gov
P.O. Box 37337
Washington, D.C. 20013
Phone: 800-444-6472

The Office of Minority Health Resource Center facilitates the exchange of information on minority health issues and serves as a national resource and referral service. The Center collects and distributes information on a broad variety of health topics, including substance abuse, cancer, heart disease, violence, diabetes, HIV/AIDS, and infant mortality.

HELPFUL WEBSITES

http://dir.yahoo.com/Social_Science/Social_Work/Organizations/Professional

This website gives a list of and links to websites for professional social work organizations.

http://www.socialworker.com/websites.htm

This website contains a comprehensive list of websites of interest for social workers and social work students.

http://www.socialworkworld.org

This website provides numerous resources, including information on recent news, education, jobs, and research.

http://cosw.sc.edu/swan/univ.html

This website provides a list of many accredited national and international schools of social work at the BSW, MSW, and PhD levels.

PRINT RESOURCES

Christensen, D.N., Todahl, J., & Barrett, W.C. (1999). *Solution-based casework: An introduction to clinical and case management skills in casework practice.* New York: Aldine de Gruyter.

Hanvey, C., & Philpot, T. (Eds.). (1994). *Practicing social work.* New York: Routledge.

Harris, J. (2003). *The social work business.* London: Routledge.

Maluccio, A.N., Pine, B.A, & Tracy, E.M. (2002). *Social work practice with families and children.* New York: Columbia University Press.

Meinert, R.G., Pardeck, J.T., & Sullivan, W.P. (Eds.). (1994). *Issues in social work: A critical analysis.* Westport, CT: Auburn House.

Vourlekis, B.S., & Greene, R.R. (1992). *Social work case management.* New York: Aldine de Gruyter.

Watts, T.D., Elliot, D., & Mayadas, N.S. (Eds.). (1995). *International handbook on social work education.* Westport, CT: Greenwood Press.

Appendix C

Sample Announcements for Casework Examinations and Open Positions

---

EXAMINATION OPEN TO THE PUBLIC

CASEWORKER
EXAM #DEC-07-17 (OC)

APPLICATIONS ACCEPTED CONTINUOUSLY

A NON-REFUNDABLE PROCESSING FEE
MUST ACCOMPANY EACH APPLICATION

$15.00 MONEY ORDER ONLY—
PAYABLE TO ONEIDA COUNTY

EXAM DATES: THIS EXAM WILL BE SCHEDULED PERIODICALLY. CANDIDATES WITH APPROVED APPLICATIONS FOR THIS EXAM WILL BE NOTIFIED BY MAIL OF THE NEXT SCHEDULED EXAM DATE.

STARTING SALARY/RANGE: $28,950 Oneida County Government   (2007)

VACANCIES: The eligible list established as a result of this examination will be used to fill this vacancy and any other appropriate vacancies which may occur in this title under the jurisdiction of the Oneida County Commissioner of Personnel.

RESIDENCE REQUIREMENT TO PARTICIPATE IN THE EXAMINATION: NONE
When preference in certification is given to residents of a municipality pursuant to sub-division 4-a of Section 23 of the Civil Service Law, an eligible candidate must have been a resident of such municipality for at least one month prior to the date of certification in order to be included in a certification as a resident of such municipality and must be a resident of such municipality at the time of appointment.

MINIMUM QUALIFICATIONS: Either:
(A) Graduation from a regionally accredited or New York State registered college or university with a Bachelor's Degree, including or supplemented by at least twelve (12) credit hours in social work, sociology, psychology, or childhood development; **OR**

(B) Graduation from a regionally accredited or New York State registered college or university with a Bachelor's Degree **AND** one (1) year of experience in social casework* with a public or private agency.

*NOTE: Social casework is defined to mean experience which shall have involved a
one-to-one interaction with a client in order to actively facilitate the identification of client
needs and goals through the interview process, as well as the development of a service
plan (i.e., identification and coordination of services available in the agency or the community to meet these needs and goals).

SUBSTITUTION: Three (3) credit hours in the areas listed in (A) above may be substituted for one (1) month of Social Casework experience.

SPECIAL REQUIREMENTS: Possession of a valid New York State driver's license at
time of application. License must remain valid throughout appointment, to meet the
transportation requirements of the job.

NOTE:
1. Applicants must meet the minimum qualifications on or before the date of the
examination.
2. Further verification may be requested from candidates to verify their academic
qualifications.
3. *Candidates* **MUST** *submit a copy of transcripts with application if qualifying under
(A) above.*

DUTIES: Responsible to provide social work services for individuals and/or their families, including children, to assist them with their economic, emotional, social, and environmental difficulties. Does related work as required.

SUBJECTS OF EXAMINATION: There will be a **PC-administered test** which you must
pass in order to be considered for appointment. The test will be administered on a personal computer (PC). Candidates need no prior knowledge of computers in order to
take the test. The test uses a simple point-and-click system that is thoroughly explained
through an animated instruction program. Candidates will be given a sample test on
which to practice before the actual test begins.

PC-administered test: This test is designed to test for knowledge, skills, and/or abilities in such areas as:
1. **Establishing and Maintaining Effective Helping Relationships in a Social
Casework Setting**—These questions test for an understanding of the factors
contributing to the development and maintenance of productive client-worker relationships. You will be provided with descriptions of specific client-worker interactions and asked to select the appropriate responses. The questions cover
such topics as confidentiality, time management, professional ethics, and referral
techniques.

2. **Interviewing (Caseworker)**—These questions test for an understanding of the principles and techniques of interviewing and their application to specific client-worker situations. You will be provided with a series of concrete interviewing situations for which you will be required to select an appropriate course of action based on an analysis of the situation, the application of the information provided, and the ramifications of various interviewing principles and strategies. You will also be asked questions about the interviewing process and various interviewing techniques.

3. **Preparing Written Material**—These questions test for the ability to present information clearly and accurately and to organize paragraphs logically and comprehensibly. For some questions, you will be given information in two or three sentences followed by four restatements of the information. You must then choose the best version. For other questions, you will be given paragraphs with their sentences out of order and then asked to choose from four suggestions the order for the sentences.

CALCULATORS ARE PERMITTED: Unless specifically prohibited, candidates are permitted to use QUIET, hand-held, solar- or battery-powered calculators ONLY. Devices with typewriter keyboards, such as cell phones, computers or devices which can be hooked up to a computer, spell-checkers, personal digital assistants, address books, language translators, dictionaries, and any similar devices are **PROHIBITED**.

NOTE: Candidates who file for Caseworker examinations with more than one civil service agency will be required to use the score received in this examination subject to the following terms and conditions:

1) A candidate is permitted to take a Caseworker examination prepared by the NYS Department of Civil Service only once during each of the following defined periods: January 1–June 30 or July 1–December 31.

2) A candidate who applies and is approved for more than one Caseworker examination during the same six-month period (January 1–June 30 or July 1–December 31) is required to use the score resulting from a single test administration for all examinations held during the same six-month period.

3) The candidate must inform the civil service agency if he/she has previously taken a Caseworker examination in any other civil service agency and provide the location and date the examination was taken.

4) A candidate must pay application fees for each examination requiring such fees.

5) A candidate's placement on resultant eligible list(s) and duration of eligibility for appointment will be determined by the civil service agency conducting the examination(s).

9579

CHILD PROTECTIVE SERVICES SUPERVISOR

NATURE OF WORK

Under general supervision, performs complex supervisory work in the provision of child protective services. Plans, assigns, and reviews the work of employees performing child protective services; performs related supervisory functions. Coordinates the work of the unit with inter- and intragovernmental units, community organizations, and advocacy groups. Work may require the use of personal automobile for travel. Employee is subject to on-call status during non-business hours. May be required to deal with situations which are potentially dangerous to client and worker. Performs related work as required.

DISTINGUISHING CHARACTERISTICS

This class is intended for positions which are assigned duties predominantly in the supervision of child protective services.

EXAMPLES OF WORK

- Plans, develops, and executes a primary mission of child protective services in a county or multi-county area through professional and para-professional staff.
- Supervises daily work of the staff.
- Develops and implements services and support programs, within regulatory and statutory guidelines.
- Maintains liaison with appropriate allied agencies and organizations.
- Serves as consultant in area of responsibility.
- Studies and recommends policy, procedures, standards, and operational methods for consideration by agency administration.
- Prepares necessary reports and records to reflect operation status of the program.
- Directs staff development activities within area of assignment.
- Evaluates effectiveness of child protective services.
- Counsels and guides professionals in the development of individual or group programs for the rehabilitation of customers.

KNOWLEDGE, SKILLS AND ABILITIES

- Knowledge of the function, organization, and regulations in child protective services.
- Knowledge of the laws and regulations underlying child protection, domestic violence, foster care, and children's mental health.
- Knowledge of the social rehabilitation process including procedures, methods, techniques, and practices with particular focus on family systems and family-centered practice.
- Knowledge of structure, functions, relationships, and practices of organizations as related to individual and family problems.
- Ability to effectively direct the work of multi-disciplinary groups in a team approach.
- Ability to establish relationships with professional and lay people at all levels.
- Ability to instruct and present ideas and information clearly and concisely, orally and in writing.
- Ability to supervise professional and para-professional staff.
- Ability to manage complex programs for the benefit of customers and the community.

MINIMUM QUALIFICATIONS

TRAINING:

Bachelor's degree in Social Work from an accredited college or university.

Substitution:

Bachelor's degree in Sociology, Psychology, Counseling, Criminal Justice, Behavioral Science, Interpersonal Communications, Human Services, Education, Special Education, Elementary Education, or Secondary Education from an accredited college or university may be substituted for the degree in Social Work.

OR

Current West Virginia Social Work License

EXPERIENCE:

Three years of full-time or equivalent part-time paid social work experience in a public or private human services agency, two years of which must have been in children's services.

Substitution:

A Master's degree in social work may substitute for one year of the required non-supervisory experience.

SPECIAL REQUIREMENT: Eligible for Temporary Social Work License **OR**

Licensed as a Social Worker, Graduate Social Worker, or Certified Social Worker by the West Virginia Board of Social Work Examiners.

PROMOTION ONLY: In addition to the Special Requirement, five years of full-time or equivalent part-time paid experience as a Social Service Supervisor, Social Service Worker, Protective Service Worker, Protective Service Worker Trainee, Family Support Specialist, or Family Support Supervisor.

Established: 12/19/01

Revised: 01/21/02, 05/02/04, 10/5/05, 02/01/2007

Effective: 02/01/2007

DISABILITY PROGRAM SPECIALIST, #H50

BASIC PURPOSE:

Positions in this job family are assigned responsibilities involving one or more of the functional disability programs in the Office of Handicapped Concerns. This may include activities related to researching disability issues, resources, and services, providing information concerning disability issues and resources to clients and others, acting as a client advocate or ombudsman, and assisting clients with resolving complaints or obtaining assistance through mediation, negotiation, or legal remedies.

TYPICAL FUNCTIONS:

The functions within this job family will vary by level, but may include the following:

- Plans, develops, implements, and coordinates various programs related to functional disabilities, including information and referral, needs assessment, employment development, or technical assistance on a statewide basis; researches disability issues, resources, and services; prepares, procures and disseminates disability issues and resource information to persons with disabilities, families, agencies, businesses, government officials, and the public.

- Performs case management and other tasks associated with the client assistance program; receives incoming requests for client assistance, identifies problems, and provides counseling, information referral, and program services to eligible for assistance.

- Provides technical assistance to disabled persons, state agencies, and political subdivisions in areas of evaluation, policies, transitional plans, architectural barriers, and cost-effective structural changes concerning compliance with federal, state, and local laws and regulations affecting persons with disabilities.

- Assists clients with civil complaints, public hearings, or other actions; pursues or assists clients in pursuing remedies to complaints through mediation, negotiation, or legal proceedings.

- Develops and conducts ongoing needs assessment studies to determine the needs of persons with disabilities; conducts special studies to identify employment related issues; analyzes data and prepares reports and recommendations.

- Collects and maintains information on employment resources; provides information, referral and counseling assistance to disabled job seekers; assists state agencies and the private sector in the development of policies and programs; coordinates, develops, and provides staff for displays, exhibitions, and awareness events throughout the state; researches, edits, and coordinates production of agency newsletters and other information materials. Organizes and conducts training workshops for individuals with disabilities, professionals, and others; coordinates and conducts presentations and meetings pertaining to the rehabilitation process.

LEVEL DESCRIPTORS:

This job family consists of four levels which are distinguished based on the level of complexity of assigned duties, the expertise required to complete assigned responsibilities, and the responsibility assigned for providing supervision to others.

Level I: Code: H50A Salary Band: I

This is the basic level of this job family where employees are assigned responsibilities involving beginning level professional work in providing assistance and information to persons with disabilities. In this role employees will receive guidance in and perform tasks related to planning, developing, implementing, and coordinating various programs involving information and referral services, needs assessment, employment development, or technical assistance.

Knowledge, Skills and Abilities required at this level include knowledge of federal, state, and municipal laws and regulations affecting programs for persons with disabilities; of available community resources for persons with disabilities; of employment problems related to various types of disabilities; of complaint procedures associated with disability problems; of interviewing techniques; of techniques used in research and investigations; and of report writing. Ability is required to read and comprehend statutes, guidelines, and other technical matter; to analyze situations and make appropriate decisions; to communicate effectively, both orally and in writing; and to establish and maintain effective working relationships with others.

Education and Experience requirements at this level consist of a bachelor's degree and one year of experience involving programs for the disabled, employment development, guidance and counseling, civil rights administration or employee relations, or an equivalent combination of education and experience, substituting one year of qualifying experience for each year of the required education.

Level II: Code: H50B Salary Band: J

This is the career level of this job family where employees are assigned responsibilities at the full performance level for a full range of duties related to developing, implementing, and coordinating various programs for persons with disabilities and providing assistance in resolving complaints or obtaining assistance through available resources.

Knowledge, Skills, and Abilities required at this level include those identified in Level I plus ability to develop and implement various programs dealing with the problems of persons with disabilities and provide technical assistance to clients and others in matters associated with disability programs and services.

Education and Experience requirements at this level consist of those identified in Level I plus one additional year of qualifying experience.

LEVEL III: CODE: H50C   SALARY BAND: K

This is the specialist level of this job family where employees are assigned responsibilities for advanced level professional work involving a wide range of issues dealing with disability programs and services. In this role, employees will primarily be involved in matters related to providing client advocacy or ombudsman services to clients and performing case management duties in providing counseling, information referral, and program services. This will also include providing assistance to clients in resolving complaints or obtaining assistance through mediation, negotiation, or legal remedies. Some responsibility may also be assigned for providing training and assistance to others.

Knowledge, Skills, and Abilities required at this level include those identified in Level II plus knowledge of grievance and legal processes; and ability is required to conduct inspections and investigations and ability to provide casework management.

Education and Experience requirements at this level consist of those identified in Level II plus one additional year of qualifying experience, including one year of experience in a program for the disabled.

LEVEL IV: CODE: H50D   SALARY BAND: L

This is the leadership level of this job family where employees are assigned responsibilities for providing supervision to others in planning, implementing, and coordinating programs and services for persons with disabilities. This will include providing guidance, training, and assistance to others, reviewing results of completed tasks and activities, and performing related administrative tasks as required.

Knowledge, Skills, and Abilities required at this level include those identified in Level III plus knowledge of supervisory principles and practices, and ability is required to supervise the work of others.

Education and Experience requirements at this level consist of those identified in Level II plus one additional year of qualifying experience in a program for the disabled.

SPECIAL REQUIREMENTS:

Applicants must be willing and able to fulfill all job related travel normally associated with this position.

Appendix D

Sample Degree Curricula

SAMPLE ASSOCIATE'S DEGREE CURRICULUM IN HUMAN SERVICES

The following curriculum is from Bronx Community College, City University of New York, which offers an associate's degree in human services:

Human Services
(A.A.S. Degree)

The A.A.S. curriculum prepares students for employment as mental health aides, group residence workers, neighborhood outreach workers, social case work assistants, geriatric counselors, assistant probation officers, and other similar positions. Employment opportunities exist in such areas as day care, mental health, social services, aging, and rehabilitation of the disabled, group and community work at the public and private level.

Graduates are prepared to pursue further education at senior colleges leading to a baccalaureate degree in several professional areas including social work, gerontology, juvenile justice, psychology, sociology, education, and counseling.

Human Services students are required to participate in two Human Services field work internships which provide supervised learning experiences in work situations. Students learn to apply theoretical material from the classroom and test career choices in the real world.

Human Services Curriculum
60 Credits required for A.A.S. Degree

Core Requirements		Credits
■ ENG 10	Fundamentals of Composition & Rhetoric OR	
ENG 11	Composition and Rhetoric I	3
■ CMS 11	Fundamentals of Interpersonal Comm.	3
■ HIS 10 or	History of the Modern World or	
HIS 11	Intro. to the Modern World	3
■ MTH 12* or	Introduction to Mathematical Thought or	
MTH 21	Survey of Mathematics I	3
■ BIO 21	The Human Body	4
	Total	16

Required Areas of Study		Credits
■ ART 11 or	Introduction to Art or	
MUS 11	Introduction to Music	3
■ ENG 12 or	Composition and Rhetoric II or	
ENG 14 or	Written Composition and Prose Fiction or	
ENG 15 or	Written Composition and Drama or	
ENG 16	Written Composition and Poetry	3
■ SOC 11	Introduction to Sociology	3
■ PSY 11	Introduction to Psychology	3
■ POL 11	American National Government	3
■ HLT 91	Critical Issues of Health	2
	Total	17

Specialization Requirements		Credits
■ HSC 10	Human Services and Social Welfare Institutions	3
■ HSC 11	Case Management	3
■ HSC 91	Field Work & Seminar in Human Services I	3
■ HSC 92	Field Work & Seminar in Human Services II	3
■ SOC 35	Introduction to Social Work	3
■ SOC 37	Class and Power in American Society	3
■ PSY 31	Abnormal Psychology	3
■ PSY 40	Life Span Development	3
■ ECO 12	Macroeconomics	3
	Total	27

*Students planning on transferring to a four-year college are advised to take MTH 21.

SAMPLE BACHELOR'S DEGREE CURRICULUM

The following curriculum is from the bachelor's program in Human Services at California State University at Fullerton:

Required Courses: (36 Units)

A. Theoretical Foundations / Intervention (9 Units)

HUSR 201	Introduction to Human Services (3)
HUSR /COUN 380	Theories and Techniques of Counseling (3)
HUSR 310	Case Management (3)

B. Client Populations / Cultural Diversity (9 Units)

HUSR / AFRO 311	Intracultural Socialization Patterns (3)
CAS 312	Human Growth and Development (3) **OR**
PSYCH 361	Developmental Psychology (3)
PSYCH 341	Abnormal Psychology (3) **OR**
SOCI 351	Sociology of the Family (3)
(formerly SOCI 451)	

C. Research / Evaluation (9 Units)

HUSR 315	Data Management in Human Services (3)
HUSR 385	Program Design & Proposal Writing (3)
	(Prerequisite: HUSR315 and HUSR 396, HUSR 396L)
HUSR 470	Evaluation of Human Services Programs (3)
	(Prerequisite: HUSR 385)

D. Skills Development / Field Experience (9 Units)

HUSR 396	Practicum Seminar (2) **AND**
HUSR 396L	Practicum (1)
	(Prerequisite: HUSR 201, HUSR 380, & HUSR 310)
HUSR 495	Fieldwork Seminar (2) **AND**
HUSR 495L	Fieldwork (1)
	(Prerequisite: HUSR 396, HUSR 396L)
HUSR 496	Internship Seminar (2) **AND**
HUSR 496L	Internship (1)
	(Prerequisite: HUSR 495, HUSR 495L)

SAMPLE CURRICULUM FROM A
BACHELOR'S SOCIAL WORK PROGRAM

The following BSW curriculum is from Ramapo College in New Jersey.

Social Work (BSW)
Requirements of the Major

Subject	Course #	Title
GENERAL EDUCATION REQUIREMENTS		
INTD	101	FIRST YEAR SEMINAR
ENGL	180	COLLEGE ENGLISH
AIID	201	READINGS IN HUMANITIES
SELECT ONE	GE—MATHEMATICS CATEGORY: MATH 101 thru 121	
SELECT ONE	GE—HISTORY: HIST 101-110	
SELECT ONE	GE—INTERCULTURAL NORTH AMERICA CATEGORY	
SELECT ONE	GE—INTERNATIONAL ISSUES CATEGORY	
SELECT ONE	GE—TOPICS ARTS AND HUMANITIES CATEGORY	
SCHOOL OF SOCIAL SCIENCE AND HUMAN SERVICES REQUIREMENTS		
SOSC	101	SOCIAL ISSUES
SOSC	235	HISTORY OF SOCIAL THOUGHT
SELECT ONE	**Consciousness and Society one course from the following:**	
EDUC	211	STUDENT LITERACY CORPS
ENST	209	WORLD SUSTAINABILITY
HIST	324	AGE OF SEGREGATION
HIST	325	THE BLACK POWER YEARS
LITR	301	LITERARY: THEORY AND CRITICISM
POLI	231	BLACK AMERICANS AND THE POLITICAL SYSTEM
POLI	360	CONFLICT RESOLUTION
POLI	327	POLITICAL PSYCHOLOGY
PSYC	306	ETHICAL AND LEGAL ISSUES
PSYC	311	PSYCHOLOGY OF GENDER
PSYC	313	VALUES IN AMERICAN CULTURE
PSYC	317	PSYCHOLOGY OF RACISM
PSYC	349	PSYCHOLOGY OF WOMEN

SOCI	205	SOCIOLOGY OF AGING
SOCI	215	SOCIOLOGY OF RACE RELATIONS
SOCI	240	THE BLACK FAMILY
SOCI	303	SOCIOLOGY OF CULTURE
SOCI	331	SOCIOLOGY OF RELIGION
SOSC	209	IDEOLOGY AND FILM
SOSC	215	AFRICAN AMERICANS IN FILM
SOSC	223	WOMEN WRITERS: MEDLEY OF VOICES
SOSC	280	WOMEN IN CONTEMPORARY SOCIETY
SOSC	308	AFRICAN AMERICAN SOCIAL AND POLITICAL THOUGHT
SWRK	330	AIDS: SOCIAL PERSPECTIVES
SELECT ONE		**History Elective (200-300 level) course from the following:**
		HIST 201-290 or HIST 301-396 or any of the following
AMER	309	HOLOCAUST & MEDIA
ENST	215	ENVIRONMENTAL HISTORY
SELECT ONE		**Social Science Elective (200-300 level) course—not in one's major**
		ANTHROPOLOGY
		ECONOMICS
		LAWS
		SOCIAL SCIENCE
		SOCIAL WORK
		SOCIOLOGY
		POLITICAL SCIENCE
		PSYCHOLOGY
		or one of the following:
EDUC	211	STUDENT LITERACY CORPS
EDUC	221	SOCIAL CONTEXT OF EDUCATION
ENST	209	WORLD SUSTAINABILITY
SELECT ONE		**Sustainability course from the following:**
ENSC	325	BIOLOGICAL CONSERVATION
ENSC	327	ECOLOGICAL AGRICULTURE
ENST	207	PUBLIC POLICY
ENST	209	WORLD SUSTAINABILITY
ENST	215	ENVIRONMENTAL HISTORY
ENST	312	ECOLOGICAL ANTHROPOLOGY
ENST	313	APPROPRIATE TECHNOLOGY
ENST	335	ECOLOGY, SOCIETY, AND THE SACRED
ENST	338	SUSTAINABLE COMMUNITIES
ENST	390	TOPICS:
GEOG	303	WATER RESOURCES
GEOG	304	FOREST RESOURCES
PSYC	343	ENVIRONMENTAL PSYCHOLOGY
SOCI	306	ENVIRONMENTAL SOCIOLOGY
SOCI	309	FOOD AND POPULATION

MAJOR REQUIREMENTS PREREQUISITES:

SOCI	101	INTRODUCTION TO SOCIOLOGY
PSYC	101	INTRODUCTION TO PSYCHOLOGY
ECON	102	INTRODUCTION TO MACROECONOMICS
SOCI	232	SOCIOLOGY OF FAMILY

SELECT ONE — **Biology Course Requirement:**

BIOL	101	INTRODUCTION TO BIOLOGY
BIOL	110	FUNDAMENTALS OF BIOLOGY I LECTURE/LAB
BIOL	213	ANATOMY AND PHYSIOLOGY I LECTURE/LAB

SOCIAL WORK PROGRAM REQUIREMENTS:

SWRK	222	HISTORY AND PHILOSOPHY OF SOCIAL WELFARE
SWRK	225	INTRODUCTION TO SOCIAL WORK
SWRK	262	HUMAN BEHAVIOR AND SOCIAL ENVIRONMENT 1—CULTURAL DIVERSITY
SWRK	263	HUMAN BEHAVIOR AND SOCIAL ENVIRONMENT 2—LIFE CYCLE
SWRK	307	SOCIAL WORK RESEARCH METHODS
SWRK	325	THEORY AND PRACTICE—SOCIAL WORK I
SWRK	326	THEORY AND PRACTICE—SOCIAL WORK II
SWRK	327	THEORY AND PRACTICE—SOCIAL WORK III
SWRK	420	CONTEMPORARY SOCIAL POLICY

SAMPLE CURRICULUM FROM A MASTER'S OF SOCIAL WORK PROGRAM

The following MSW curriculum is from Binghamton University's Department of Social Work:

Full-Time Students

Professional Foundation

Fall Semester—Year 1

SW 501	Human Behavior in the Social Environment I	3 credits
SW 510	Generalist Social Work Practice I	3 credits
SW 515	Social Welfare Policy and Programs	3 credits
SW 500	Research Methods in Social Work	3 credits
SW 591	Field Instruction I	4 credits

Spring Semester—Year 1

SW 502	Human Behavior in the Social Environment II	3 credits
SW 511	Generalist Social Work Practice II	3 credits
SW 512	Generalist Social Work Practice III	3 credits
SW 503	Diversity and Oppression	3 credits
SW 592	Field Instruction II	4 credits

Advanced Generalist Concentration

Fall Semester—Year 2

SW 521	Advanced Social Work Practice with Individuals	3 credits
SW 522	Advanced Social Work Practice with Organizations	3 credits
SW 520	Evaluation of Social Work Practice	3 credits
SW XXX	Elective	3 credits
SW 593	Field Instruction III	4 credits

Spring Semester—Year 2

SW 523	Advanced Social Work Practice with Groups	3 credits
SW 524	Advanced Social Work Practice with Families	3 credits
SW 525	Advanced Social Work Practice with Communities	3 credits
SW XXX	Elective	3 credits
SW 594	Field Instruction IV	4 credits

Curriculum for Part-Time Students

Professional Foundation

Fall—Year 1

SW 501	Human Behavior in the Social Environment I	3 credits
SW 510	Generalist Social Work Practice I	3 credits

Spring—Year 1

SW 502	Human Behavior in the Social Environment II	3 credits
SW 500	Research Methods in Social Work	3 credits

Summer—Year 1

SW 515	Social Welfare Policy and Programs	3 credits
SW 511	Generalist Social Work Practice II	3 credits

Fall—Year 2

SW 503	Diversity and Oppression	3 credits
SW 591	Field Instruction I	4 credits

Spring—Year 2

SW 512	Generalist Social Work Practice III	3 credits
SW 592	Field Instruction II	4 credits

Advanced Generalist Concentration

Summer—Year 2

SW 524	Advanced Social Work Practice with Families	3 credits
SW 523	Advanced Social Work Practice with Groups	3 credits

Fall—Year 3

SW 521	Advanced Social Work Practice with Individuals	3 credits
SW 522	Advanced Social Work Practice with Organizations	3 credits

Spring—Year 3

SW XXX	Elective	3 credits
SW 525	Advanced Social Work Practice with Communities	3 credits

Summer—Year 3

SW XXX	Elective	3 credits
SW 593	Field Instruction III	4 credits

Fall—Year 4

SW 520	Evaluation of Social Work Practice	3 credits
SW 594	Field Instruction IV	4 credits

References

American Academy of Child and Adolescent Psychiatry. 2004. *The depressed child.* Retrieved November 25, 2007, from http://www.aacap .org/cs/root/facts_for_families/the_depressed_child.

American Public Health Association. n.d., a. *What is public health?* Retrieved February 10, 2008, from http://www.apha.org/NR/ rdonlyres/C57478B8-8682-4347-8DDF-A1E24E82B919/0/what_is_ PH_May1_Final.pdf.

American Public Health Association. n.d., b. *APHA: Priorities.* Retrieved November 22, 2007, from http://www.apha.org/advocacy/priorities.

Association of Social Work Boards. n.d. *Table 2: Levels of Practice Regulated.* Retrieved December 10, 2007, from http://www.datapathdesign.com.

Barker, R.L. 1995. *The social work dictionary.* Washington, D.C.: NASW Press.

Bloom, M. 1996. *Primary prevention practices.* Thousand Oaks, CA: Sage Publications.

Britain, C.H., and D. Hunt. 2004. *Helping in child protective services: A competency-based casework handbook.* New York: Oxford University Press.

Burns, D.D. 1980. *Feeling good: The new mood therapy.* New York: Morrow.

Care Pathways. 2008. *Nursing home services.* Retrieved February 29, 2008, from http://www.carepathways.com/NHx1.cfm.

Centers for Medical & Medicaid Services. 2007. *Managed care in Medicaid.* Retrieved February 29, 2008, from http://www.cms.hhs.gov/Medicaid ManagCare/.

Child Welfare Information Gateway. 2006. *Child abuse and neglect fatalities: Statistics and interventions.* Retrieved November 24, 2007, from http://www.childwelfare.gov/pubs/factsheets/fatality.cfm.

Child Welfare Information Gateway. n.d. *Shaken baby syndrome.* Retrieved January 14, 2008, from http://www.childwelfare.gov/can/types/physical abuse/shaken.cfm.

Cohen, J.A. 2003. Managed care and the evolving role of the clinical social worker in mental health. *Social Work, 48*(1), 34–43.

Comas-Díaz, L., and F.M. Jacobsen. 1991. Ethnocultural transference and countertransference in the therapeutic dyad. *American Journal of Orthopsychiatry, 61*(3), 392–402.

Coulton, C.J. 1990. Research in patient and family decision making regarding life sustaining and long term care. *Social Work in Health Care, 15*(1), 63–78.

Council of State Governments. n.d. *Public health issues.* Retrieved November 23, 2007, from http://www.healthystates.csg.org/Public+Health+Issues.

Council of State Governments. 2004. *HIV and AIDS.* Retrieved November 23, 2007, from http://www.healthystates.csg.org/Public+Health+Issues/HIV+and+AIDS.

Council on Social Work Education. 2001. *Accreditation.* Retrieved December 2, 2007, from http://www.cswe.org/CSWE/accreditation.

Cowles, L.A. 2000. *Social work in the health field.* New York: Haworth Press.

Cross, T. 2003. Foreword. In D. Lum, ed. *Culturally competent practice.* Sacramento, CA: Thomson Brooks/Cole, vi–viii.

Dhooper, S.S. 1997. *Social work in health care in the 21st century.* Thousand Oaks, CA: Sage Publications.

Downs, S.W., E. Moore, E.J. McFadden, S. Michaud, and L.B. Costin. 2004. *Child welfare and family services: Policies and practice.* Boston: Pearson A and B.

Dziegielewski, S.F. 2004. *The changing face of health care social work: Professional practice in managed behavioral health care, 2nd ed.* New York: Springer.

Fassinger, R.E. 1991. The hidden minority: Issues and challenges in working with lesbian women and gay men. *Counseling Psychologist, 19*(2), 157–176.

Germain, C. 1970. Casework and science: A historical encounter. In R.R. Roberts and R.H. Nee, eds. *Theories of social casework.* Chicago: University of Chicago Press.

Gordon, T. 1975. *Parent effectiveness training: The tested new way to raise responsible children.* New York: Penguin.

Hepworth, D.H., R.H. Rooney, G.D. Rooney, K. Strom-Gotterfried, and J. Larsen. 2006. *Direct social work practice: Theory and skills, 7th ed.* Belmont, CA: Thomson, Brooks/Cole.

Himmelstein, D.U., S. Woolhandler, J. Hellender, and S.M. Wolfe. 1999. Quality of care in investor-owned vs. not-for-profit HMOs. *Journal of the American Medical Association, 282*(2), 159–163.

Holland, T.P., and A.C. Kilpatrick. 1991. Ethical issues in social work: Toward a grounded theory of professional ethics. *Social Work, 36*(2), 138–144.

Hurley, R., and D.A. Draper. 1998. Medicaid managed care for special need populations: Behavioral health as "tracer condition." In D. Mechanic, ed. *Managed behavioral health care: Current realities and future potential* (pp. 51–65). San Francisco: Jossey Bass Publishers.

Job Accommodation Network. 1997. *ADA: A brief overview.* Retrieved November 24, 2007, from http://www.jan.wvu.edu/links/adasummary.htm.

Kadushin, A., and G. Kadushin, 1997. *The social work interview: A guide for human service professionals.* New York: Columbia University Press.

Keigher, S.M. 1997. What role for social work in the new health care practice paradigm? *Health and Social Work, 22*(2), 149–155.

Kiesler, C.A. 1992. U.S. mental health policy: Doomed to failure. *American Psychologist, 47*(9), 1077–1082.

LaRoche, M.J., and C. Turner. 2002. At the crossroads: Managed mental health care, the ethics code, and ethnic minorities. *Cultural Diversity and Ethnic Minority Psychology, 8*(3), 187–198.

Lum, D. 2003. *Culturally competent practice: A framework for understanding diverse groups and justice issues.* Belmont, CA: Thomson, Brooks/Cole.

Lum, D. 2005. *Cultural competence, practice stages, and client systems: A case study approach.* Belmont, CA: Thomson, Brooks/Cole.

Mattaini, M. 2002. Practice with individuals. In Mattaini, M.A., C.T. Lowery, and C.H. Meyer, eds. *Foundations of social work practice.* Washington, D.C.: NASW, 151–183.

McFarland, B.H. 1994. Health maintenance organizations and persons with severe mental illness. *Community Mental Health Journal, 30*(3), 221–242.

McFarland, B.H. 1996. Ending the millennium: Commentary on "HMOs and the seriously mentally ill—a view from the trenches." *Community Mental Health Journal, 32*(3), 219–222.

Mechanic, D. 2001. Lessons from the unexpected: The importance of data infrastructure, conceptual models, and serendipity in health services research. *The Millbank Quarterly, 79*(3) 459–477.

Mechanic, D. 2002. Socio-cultural implications of changing organizational technologies in the provision of care. *Social Science and Medicine, 54*(3), 459–467.

Mechanic, D. 1999. *Mental health and social policy. The emergence of managed care.* Boston: Allyn & Bacon.

Mechanic, D., and D.D. McAlpine. 1999. Mission unfulfilled: Potholes on the road to mental health parity. *Teaching Health Affairs, 18*(5), 7–21.

Mechanic, D., M. Schlesinger, and D.D. McAlpine. 1995. Management of mental health and substance abuse services: State of the art and early results. *The Milbank Quarterly, 73*(1), 19–55.

National Association of Social Workers. n.d. *Practice.* Retrieved November 15, 2007, from http://www.socialworkers.org/practice.

National Association of Social Workers. 1999. *Code of ethics.* Retrieved November 15, 2007, from http://www.socialworkers.org/pubs/code/code.asp.

National Association of Social Workers. 2003. *Practice Research Network (PRN).* Retrieved November 15, 2007, from http://www.socialworkers .org/naswprn/surveyTwo/Datagram1.pdf.

National Association of Social Workers. 2005. *NASW standards for social work practice in health care settings.* Retrieved November 20, 2007, from http://www.socialworkers.org/practice/standards/NASWHealthCare Standards.pdf.

National Association of Social Workers. 2006. *Social work speaks: National Association of Social Workers policy statements 2003–2006.* Washington, D.C.: NASW Press.

National Center on Shaken Baby Syndrome. n.d., a. *About us.* Retrieved January 14, 2008, from http://dontshake.com/subject.aspx?CategoryID=3.

National Center on Shaken Baby Syndrome. n.d., b. *Physical signs/symptoms.* Retrieved January 14, 2008, from http://dontshake.com/Audience.aspx?categoryID=7&PageName=SymptomsOfSBS.htm.

National Institute of Mental Health. 2007. *Attention deficit hyperactivity disorder.* Retrieved November 24, 2007, from http://www.nimh.nih.gov/health/publications/adhd/complete-publication.shtml.

National Institute on Drug Abuse (n.d.). *Preventing drug abuse among children and adolescents.* Retrieved January 14, 2008, from http://www.drugabuse.gov/prevention/risk.html.

Othmer, E., and S.C. Othmer. 1989. *The clinical interview using DSM-IV: Volume 1, fundamentals.* Washington, D.C.: American Psychiatric Press.

Packard, T. 1989. Participation in decision-making, performance, and job satisfaction in a social work bureaucracy. *Administration in Social Work, 13*(1), 59–73.

Potter-Efron, R.T., and P.S. Potter-Efron. 2006. *Letting go of anger.* Oakland, CA: New Harbinger Publications.

Public Health Foundation. n.d. Public health infrastructure resource center.

Reamer, F.G. 1998. *Ethical standards in social work: A critical review of the NASW code of ethics.* Washington, D.C.: NASW Press.

Richmond, M.E. 1917. *Social diagnosis.* New York: Russell Sage Foundation.

Rothbard, A.B., A.P. Schinnar, T.R. Hadley, and J.I. Rovi. 1990. Integration of mental health data on hospital and community services. *Administration and Policy in Mental Health, 18*(2), 91–99.

Sands, R.G. 2001. *Clinical social work practice in behavioral mental health: A postmodern approach to practice with adults.* Boston: Allyn & Bacon, 27–46.

Shapiro, J. 1995. The downside of managed mental health care. *Clinical Social Work Journal, 2*(4), 441–451.

Sherwood, D.A. 1989. Spiritual assessment as a normal part of social work practice: Power to help and power to harm. *Social Work and Christianity, 25*(2), 80–90.

Schwartz, W. 1971. On the use of groups in social work practice. In W. Schwartz and S. Zalba, eds. *The practice of group work.* New York: Columbia University Press, 3–24.

Shulman, L. 2005. *The skills of helping individuals, families, groups, and communities.* Florence, KY: Wadsworth/Cengage Learning.

Sullivan, K. 1999. Managed care plan performance since 1980: Another look at 2 literature reviews. *American Journal of Public Health, 89*(7), 1003–1008.

Sunley, R. 1997. Advocacy in the new world of managed care. *Families in Society: The Journal of Contemporary Human Services, 78*(1), 184–194.

Summers, N. 2006. *Fundamentals of case management practice: Skills for the human services.* Belmont, CA: Thomson Brooks/Cole.

United States Census Bureau. 2007. *Health Insurance Coverage: 2006.* Retrieved February 29, 2008, from http://www.census.gov/hhes/www/hlthins/hlthins.html.

United States Department of Health & Human Services. 2003. *Summary of the HIPAA privacy rule.* Retrieved November 20, 2007, from http://www.hhs.gov/ocr/privacysummary.pdf.

United States Department of Health & Human Services. 2006. *Office of Family Assistance.* Retrieved November 26, 2007, from http://www.acf.hhs.gov/opa/fact_sheets/tanf_factsheet.html.

United States Department of Housing and Urban Development. n.d. *Housing choice vouchers fact sheet.* Retrieved November 26, 2007, from http://www.hud.gov/offices/pih/programs/hcv/about/fact_sheet.cfm.

United States Department of Labor. n.d. *Social assistance, except child day care.* Retrieved November 29, 2007, from http://www.bls.gov/oco/cg/cgs040.htm.

United States Senate Special Committee on Aging. n.d. *Improving and expanding long term care.* Retrieved November 23, 2007, from http://aging.senate.gov/issues/longterm/index.cfm.

Weaver, H.N. 1999. Indigenous peoples and the social work profession: Defining culturally competent services. *Social Work, 44*(3), 217–225.

World Health Organization. n.d. *HIV infections.* Retrieved November 23, 2007, from http://www.who.int/topics/hiv_infections/en.

World Health Organization. 1958. Constitution of the World Health Organization. In *The first ten years of the world health organization.* Geneva: World Health Organization, 459–472.